PRACTICAL IDEAS FOR MULTI-CULTURAL LEARNING AND TEACHING IN THE PRIMARY CLASSROOM

Ruth Hessari and Dave Hill

Foreword by Lord Swann

ROUTLEDGE

First published 1989
by Routledge
11 New Fetter Lane, London EC4P 4EE
Reprinted 1990

Filmset by Mayhew Typesetting, Bristol, England
Printed and bound in Great Britain by
Biddles Ltd, Guildford and King's Lynn

British Library Cataloguing in Publication Data

Hessari, Ruth
  Practical ideas for multi-cultural learning
  and teaching in the primary classroom.
  1. Great Britain. Primary Schools.
  Multicultural education
  I. Title   II. Hill, Dave, *1945–*
  372'.011'5
  ISBN 0–415–03908–8
      0–415–03641–0 (pbk.)

Dedication

We should like to dedicate this book to Dick Chester, of Claremont Primary School, Nottingham, who died tragically in March 1988. Ruth met him only briefly, but his work vividly illustrated for her the dynamism and excitement of a truly multi-cultural classroom. The work he was doing with his class, and its influence within the whole school, made a great impact on her, and brought into sharp focus all of the many facets that go towards making a good education for all of our children within our multi-cultural society.

Dick Chester's sensitive perceptions have spread outwards from his own school, and we hope that parts of this book have captured a little of his commitment, enthusiasm, and professionalism for other teachers to experience.

Ruth Hessari
Dave Hill

Contents

viii   Contents

Foreword

In 1981 I took on the chairmanship of a large government committee with a widely mixed membership. Our job was to consider the problems of Britain's ethnic minorities, and to make recommendations about the contribution that the educational system could make towards their solution. It took us four years, and in 1985 our massive report was finally published. It was, inevitably, the best consensus that the committee could reach, and I don't suppose for a moment that every member of the committee agreed with everything it said. Certainly I didn't. Nevertheless, it was welcomed by the government of the day, and I would like to think that it has subsequently acted as a worthwhile stimulus to the teaching profession.

Some readers of this book will no doubt have looked at the report, though I doubt whether many of them will have read all 800 pages. Its length led Sir Keith Joseph, Secretary of State at the time, to ask me at the last minute to write myself what he called a brief guide to the main issues of the report. This was published separately, and once again I don't suppose that every member of the committee agreed with everything I said.

A foreword is hardly the place to summarize even a summary, but the title that we finally chose for the main report, *Education for All*, is enough to convey the general drift, namely that the problem is not just one of improving the education of ethnic minority children, but working towards methods of education that would lead in the long run to the elimination of racially prejudiced views on the part of the white majority.

The committee did not attempt to spell things out in great detail. The problems are far too subtle and complex for any committee to be able to lay down hard and fast agreed rules. But we did hope that teachers far and wide would develop their own ideas, and that gradually it would become apparent what worked best. Our hopes were perhaps spelt out most effectively by one member of the committee, James Cornford, Director of the Nuffield Foundation at the time, at the end of an Annex he wrote on the pressing need for more research. This is what he said:

> Many of the recommendations of this report are, as it were, acts of faith, based upon experience and common sense. If as we hope, they are implemented, they will become hypotheses to be tested to see whether or not they have the good results we expect.

The authors of this book have moved in just the direction that we hoped teachers would move. They have worked out their own methods in detail and are trying them out. I have never taught in a school, and I cannot comment with any authority on what they propose. But people who can, are impressed. I only hope that Hessari and Hill's ideas will prove fruitful, and still more, since there is no monopoly of wisdom in this area, that they and their book will stimulate others to do likewise.

Michael Swann

Acknowledgements

We should like to thank the staff and children of all of the schools whose work we saw, in particular the following:

Bewbush First, Crawley, West Sussex
Claremont Primary and Nursery, Nottingham
Croft Nursery, Nottingham
Crossdale Primary, Keyworth, Nottinghamshire
Culloden Infants, Tower Hamlets, London
Edna G. Oldes Primary and Nursery, Nottingham
Elms Primary and Nursery, Nottingham
Greenwood Junior, Sneinton, Nottingham
Hangleton Infants, Hove, East Sussex
Hertford Junior, Brighton, East Sussex
Kings Acre Junior, Brixton, London
Langley Green Middle, Crawley, West Sussex
Middle Street Primary and Nursery, Brighton, East Sussex
Milford Primary and Nursery, Clifton, Nottingham
Seagrave Primary and Nursery, Strelley, Nottingham
Snapewood Primary, Bulwell, Nottingham
St Anne's Well Infants and Nursery, Nottingham
St John the Baptist C. of E. Primary, Hackney, London
Stanley Junior, Nottingham
Westdale Junior, Carlton, Nottingham

We should also like to thank officers of the following LEAs for their help during discussions: Birmingham, Derbyshire, East Sussex, ILEA, Kent, Leicestershire, Nottinghamshire, and West Sussex. Thanks also to Andrea Wells for her indefatigable and good-humoured typing, and to Jack Dranse for his patient proof-reading. Photographs in this book are by the authors and by Susan Elliott of West Sussex Institute of Higher Education.

The views expressed in this book are our own and should not be attributed to any others.

Glossary

All-white areas Denotes areas of this country where the vast majority of the people regard themselves as 'white'. The term is inexact, in that very few parts of Britain now have only white people and, even there, a look into the past would often reveal a mixture of cultures within most 'native' Britons. It is used here for want of a better term and because it is commonly used.

Black and Asian Britons Can include all people except those who would describe themselves as white. It is an inadequate label, objected to by some, as it gives no indication of the variety that is included in it: for example, the large number of countries covered by the word 'Asia' or the variations in culture between black Africans and black Afro-Caribbeans.

Culture All that goes to make up the detail of the lives of varied groups of people: learned behaviour, such as values, attitudes, and beliefs; material aspects, such as clothes, diet, housing; language; religion; relationships. It is dynamic and ever-changing.

Hidden curriculum All aspects of school life which are not directly taught but which are absorbed by contact: for example, attitudes, prejudices, stereotypes, the subtle influences of omissions. These are often apparent in the parts of school life that are not directly concerned with 'lessons': in the atmosphere within the school; in the attitude towards parents, visitors, ancillaries; in the organization of the 'caring' side of the school; in the whole human context of the school.

Mono-cultural Acknowledging aspects of only one culture, in this case white culture, and often ignoring the variety within even that single culture.

Multi-cultural, ethnically diverse   These, and other forms of these words, are used interchangeably here. They refer to all of the possible cultures and culture-mixes that make up British society. These cultures include European, Welsh, Scottish, Irish, Celtic, Travellers', Eastern European, as well as the diversity included in the terms Black and Asian.

Part I Introduction

1. Background information

Rationale and Structure

We use the terms 'multi-cultural education' and 'education for ethnic diversity' interchangeably throughout this book, therefore it is essential to define them. Our concept of multi-cultural education, or education for ethnic diversity, could be written as 'multi-cultural/anti-racist education'. We conceive it to be that which enables children to develop towards maturity with the ability to recognize inequality, injustice, racism, stereotypes, prejudice, and bias, and which equips them with the knowledge and skills to help them to challenge and try to change these manifestations when they encounter them in all strata of society.

We have written this book in the firm belief that multi-cultural education (as we define it), which is fully integrated into the whole life of schools, enables all of the commonly accepted aims of good education to be achieved for *all* of our children. We would go further and say that education that is not multi-cultural (albeit good in other aspects) is, however unintentionally, narrow, racist, and biased. It encourages our children to be satisfied with less than the truth and is therefore innately incapable of being a good education. We are fully supported in this belief by documents such as *The National Curriculum: From Policy to Practice* (1989), the Swann Report, *Education for All* (1985), the Scarman Report (1981), and numerous Local Education Authority policy documents.

We also believe that education for ethnic diversity is not an optional extra which teachers may choose to include or omit a belief which has now been made a statutory requirement through National Curriculum legislation. As we stress throughout the book, we see multi-cultural education neither as a separate subject, to be slotted into the existing timetable, nor as a completely new method of teaching but as an extension, a development, a deepening of all of the often excellent teaching and learning that is going on in many schools.

There are six assumptions underlying this book:

1 Education for ethnic diversity is no more and no less than a good education for *all* children in our very diverse, multi-cultural society. It aims to open children's minds to the facts, rather than the suppositions, of diversity within ourselves, within others, within this and every national society.

2 Education for ethnic diversity can and should be an integral part not only of all of the generally acknowledged school skills and concepts but also of those skills, concepts, and attitudes that children need out of school. These include: skills in co-operating, sharing, empathizing, fact-finding, communicating, questioning, thinking, and recognizing bias and prejudice; concepts of unity, interdependence, and causality; attitudes of mind which value fairness, tradition, change, and curiosity, and which understand and can handle conflict, power, and differences. These are the goals to be worked towards, in line with the recommendations of, among others, the Swann Report, *Education for All*, the HMI document, *Curriculum 5–16*, the current Committee for the Accreditation of Teacher Education concerning requirements for teacher training, and most of the 104 Local Education Authorities in England and Wales which have produced multi-cultural policies.

3 Ethnically diverse education can and should be taught through all of school life – through all the 'ordinary' work of the children and all parts of the 'hidden' curriculum – and not through special 'one-off' topics, a view endorsed by the National Curriculum documents. A topic on India or Islam might have a place in a school which practises multi-cultural education but, when slotted into a curriculum that is mono-cultural, it will be viewed as strange, exotic, foreign, and concerning 'them out there' rather than 'us here'. It can too easily be seen as irrelevant and may do little for children's understanding and awareness of the multi-cultural nature of our own society.

4 The process of education is important, not just the product.

The photographs in this book quite clearly show the 'product' of some degree of multi-cultural teaching. Such a product may or may not be the result of much learning. The purpose of this book is to achieve skills, and attitude and cognitive development, rather than simply a nice wall display.

5 Cultures are dynamic and changing. All cultures, as they interact with others either by migration or conquest, alter continually. For example, the cultures of first-generation Italians or Bangladeshis who are living in Britain differ in detail from the cultures not only of Italy or Bangladesh but also of future generations of their descendants. 'British' culture is likewise continually altering and adapting.

6 Cultures are not as monolithic or homogeneous as is often assumed. The convenient labels that we use hide an enormous variation within them. For example, the blanket label 'African' encloses many nations, cultures, religions, and languages and tries to impose a camouflaging, even patronizing unity over a vast, diverse land mass. British culture is equally diverse, encompassing regional and ethnic cultures, such as Scottish, Irish, Welsh, 'Northern', and Travellers', and social class sub-cultures. It is also developmental, having been influenced in past and present by conquerors, by political and religious refugees, and by economic immigration.

Although the book is written with children in all-white schools and areas particularly in mind, it may be used by any primary school teacher because multi-cultural education is not a different entity depending on where people live. The book chiefly deals with the practical applications of multi-cultural education in the primary school. It endeavours to show both how stimulating this approach is to all of school life and the enormous amount of rich, varied material that can be employed to achieve the aim of a multi-cultural/anti-racist education.

The book demonstrates how primary teachers can develop the work that they are already presenting to the children by including British ethnic and cultural diversity, and influences from the rest of the world, within that work. It shows that virtually all work which goes on in schools can contain multi-cultural elements, in the broadest sense of that term. Thus, once teachers begin to bear in mind the aims and objectives of multi-cultural education, they can positively broaden their approach and easily adapt their present practices to extend the education in which the children participate. It also emphasizes that education for ethnic diversity is not a separate area of the timetable, operating within clearly defined parameters; to make it a fully accepted, normal part of life, it must not be distinguishable from everything else that constitutes a good education for all of our children. This is also the view of the Department of Education and Science, expressed in *The National Curriculum: From Policy to Practice*. 'The foundation subjects are certainly *not* a complete curriculum; . . . the *whole* curriculum for *all* pupils will certainly need to include at appropriate (and in some cases all) stages . . . coverage across the curriculum of . . . multi-cultural issues.' Such areas 'are clearly required in the curriculum which all pupils are entitled to by virtue of section 1 of the [1988 Education] Act. . . . Some elements will certainly be contained in the attainment targets and programmes of study' (para. 3.8). [Original emphasis throughout]

The book is planned as a collection of ideas and stimuli which primary school teachers and student teachers can take, add to, and utilize as they want. It is intended to be used as a collection not of plans of work but of starting points which a teacher will develop into work for children which is unique to that teacher, that class, and that time. It is hoped that the material is sufficiently adaptable for teachers to fulfil their own classroom aims and objectives through it.

The book uses topic work as the vehicle for most of the taught aspects of multi-cultural education. Topic work relies on teachers drawing the content of the curriculum areas that they are teaching from one central focus, rather than dealing with the subject areas in isolation. The focus can be infinitely variable, to suit the children, the teacher, the season, events out of school, etc. Thus, a good primary school teacher can cover curriculum aims and objectives through topic themes with titles ranging from 'Food' and 'Frogs' to 'Fashion' and 'Families'. This method of teaching can firmly establish the fundamental relationships between all areas of the curriculum. It relies heavily on continuity, while demonstrating an enormous breadth within that continuity. It is therefore an ideal way to deal with multi-cultural education, which is founded on an amalgam of all areas of life that is so thorough that it cannot be separated off into discrete packages of learning. Indeed, *The National Curriculum: From Policy to Practice* specifically recognizes teaching through topic work as a major method of organizing the curriculum, by which core and foundation subjects, and cross-curricular areas, such as multicultural education, can be fully integrated (para. 4.8).

The book is arranged in two parts. The first sets out the thinking behind the book, and takes a brief look outwards towards a deeper understanding of education for ethnic diversity. The second contains the practical ideas for classroom usage.

The second part of the book divides multi-cultural education into three spheres: Themes for topic work, Aspects of personal and social development, and Strands of interweaving components. These divisions have been made only for clarity of presentation and not because we see education for ethnic diversity in practice as being in discrete parts. On the contrary, the essence of multi-cultural education is that it permeates all that happens in schools, and that the constituent parts of multi-cultural education are inseparably linked. Thus, a topic which was developed from some of the ideas in the Themes would consist of areas of the curriculum subjects, which in turn would contain Aspects of personal and social development, and elements from the spheres that are covered by the Strands.

The main topic web on p. 48 'Ourselves', shows how the Themes for topic work, and the Aspects of personal and social development, are directly related to the children and the world in which they live. The areas which are covered by the Strands weave inseparably throughout all of the topic web.

The book is essentially a resource of ideas to stimulate fresh interests and thoughts that will augment well-used topics, and to indicate how attitudes, concepts, and skills can be developed through them. However, it is not intended to give the impression that these school learning and teaching activities are all that concerns education for ethnic diversity. Such activities are certainly an important part of it but are by no means the whole story. Other aspects of multi-cultural education are briefly looked at below.

Teacher awareness and the training of teachers to be aware of racism, bias, stereotyping, and prejudice within our society in general and ourselves in particular are essential requirements to bring about change in practice. If the practical suggestions in this book are adopted without teachers being aware of why they are suggested and without their being able to see the many subtleties involved, the intended aims and objectives will almost certainly not be achieved. It is therefore most important that the ideas which are offered here are used by teachers in conjunction with positive efforts to inform themselves, though reading, thinking, talking, and attending training courses, of the deeper aims and objectives of multi-cultural and anti-racist education. (See Chapter 2 for more details of the educational theories and literature.) The practical suggestions in this book can serve as only one of many vehicles which can be used to move towards the goal of a just, fair, and unprejudiced society.

Individual teachers, who are integrating multi-cultural and anti-racist aspects into their work, are important in the overall spread of education for ethnic diversity. However, good practice which abruptly stops outside one or two classroom doors will obviously not be as effective as that which embraces the whole school.

It would be ideal if everybody involved in a school – teachers, ancillaries, cleaners, caretakers, school meals staff, governors, parents – could work together raising their awareness and could then write an agreed policy for multi-cultural and anti-racist education. They could put it into practice and monitor, evaluate, and change it. However, this is not always a possible starting point. Teachers will often feel unable to obtain agreement within the whole school. This should not deter them from changing their own practice but the goal of a whole school policy must stay firmly in view.

Although individual schools which embrace multi-cultural and anti-racist education are important, the whole spectrum of this aspect of education, in order to be really effective, requires a commitment from LEAs to provide training and resources, and to undertake the review and change of practices through-out the sphere of their influence.

Much has been written elsewhere on these areas of multi-cultural and anti-racist education. It is hoped that this book will help to offset the comparative lack of published material available on primary classroom practice for integrating multi-cultural aspects into children's work.

Historical perspective

Multi-cultural and anti-racist education have evolved over a period of time, adapting Britain's ethnocentric education to respond first to the problems met by 'immigrant' children and later to an increasing awareness of the multi-cultural nature of society and of the racism operating through all levels of that society.

Assimilation

The seeds of the concept of multi-cultural and anti-racist education for all of our children have their unlikely origins in the crudely insensitive, assimilationist theories which developed gradually from the longheld, unthinking expectation that all 'foreigners' would forget their own backgrounds and cultures, learn to speak English, and thus become British. By the late 1950s, this common expectation had developed into a firm theory of assimilation, to enable the education system to cope with the steadily increasing numbers of so-called immigrant children entering our schools. The number of children born in this country to immigrant parents was also increasing

The numbers of these children grew quite rapidly because changes in the immigration laws in the 1960s forced men to bring their families to Britain or else have them permanently excluded. Prior to this period, most ethnic minority workers (many of whom, incidentally, had been invited to come by the Government during the boom years after the Second World War) expected to return to their families in their countries of origin after a period of working in Britain.

The policy of assimilation was given further official credence in 1965 by a DES circular which recommended 'dispersal' of 'immigrant children': a practice which became known as 'bussing'. Children of immigrants, or at any rate those of black and Asian immigrants, were perceived as having problems, and as causing difficulties in the schools that they attended; the solution to their problems was considered to be their rapid assimilation into the British way of life. Having too many 'immigrant' children in one school was therefore seen as undesirable because they diluted the culture on which they were to remodel themselves and thus caused their 'problems' to last longer than necessary. It was recommended that no school should let the numbers of 'immigrant' children rise above one-third of the total number of children. To achieve this target, 'immigrant' children were 'bussed' to white schools outside their neighbourhoods.

No thought was directed inwards at this time to see whether British society and our school system might be causing these difficulties or, indeed, whether the difficulties might be caused by unacknowledged problems within the majority white British population.

The policy of 'bussing' was not officially abandoned until 1973. Although many LEAs had never adopted it, it was 1979 before the last participating LEA did stop 'bussing' children.

Integration

In 1966 the term 'integration' was defined in a speech by Roy Jenkins. By the end of the 1960s, the move towards integration in education was gaining ground.

The integrationist theory considered that a culturally homogeneous society could be created as a result of the immigrants adapting and changing their ways sufficiently to fit in with the white culture. However, they were no longer expected to shed their own cultures completely, and the white majority was expected to tolerate some differences between the cultures.

At around this time, the term 'ethnic minorities' began to replace that of 'immigrants'.

Although ethnic minority children were still regarded as 'problems', it was gradually being recognized in some quarters that it was racism within our society that was contributing to many of the problems being experienced by ethnic minority children. Generally, however, the host white communities still did not recognize any faults in themselves as the causes of the difficulties that these children were experiencing.

Schools and teachers were beginning to amass a certain expertise in meeting the needs of ethnic minority children, including the ability to integrate the children better into the existing mainstream schooling. However, the need to alter this mainstream schooling (for example, the content of the ethnocentric curriculum) for all children was still not recognized.

Cultural pluralism and multi-cultural education

During the 1970s, the broadly similar terms 'multi-racial', 'multi-ethnic', and 'multi-cultural' gained currency and the theory of cultural pluralism began to spread. This envisaged a society which was socially cohesive but culturally diverse. Its aim was that every Briton should hold a unified view of his/her social obligations and rights, while upholding individuals' rights to their own culture, within the confines of a common law. It also acknowledged that culture is essentially a changing phenomenon, and that most people's culture would adopt certain strands from the cultures of other communities.

This period saw increasing acknowledgement of the facts that our white, ethnocentric and racist culture was creating problems for the ethnic minority communities, that much was wrong with our view of the world, and that our values and attitudes needed to be re-assessed. The positive values of bilingualism and of a culturally mixed society were also beginning to be recognized.

In 1985, the long-awaited publication of the Swann Report gave official, national legitimation to cultural pluralism and to multi-cultural education. Since then the Government has supported some developments in this field at local level with, for example, education support grants (ESGs). The LEA response to multi-cultural education has been and still is hugely varied, both in commitment and in resourcing.

The term 'education for ethnic diversity' gained popularity following the appearance of the Swann Report. Today all four of these terms are used here.

Anti-racism in education

Throughout the 1970s, a more radical theory of the changes needed within education and, more importantly, within society was being developed. This was anti-racism, which is concerned with more than education within schools. Anti-racism sees institutional inequality, such as institutional racism, as the hub of the inequality of our society. Institutional racism is widely believed to be built, sometimes unconsciously and unintentionally, into the very fabric of society and it results in discrimination in all areas of life against black and

Asian Britons and people from other minority cultures. Anti-racists believe that this must be recognized and eradicated before society as a whole can become more equal. They see racism in all its forms as a solely white problem; anything that does not directly attack this, such as multi-cultural education, is mere tinkering at the edges of the problem.

The late 1980s are seeing a backlash, particularly against anti-racist, but also against multi-cultural, education. The policies which were developed by some LEAs have been distorted by the popular media and portrayed as being dangerous and destabilizing for society. The reaction to the *Macdonald Report* on Burnage High School in Manchester, and the attempt (however short-lived) of Berkshire LEA to rescind its seminal *Policy Statement on Racial Equality and Justice* are good illustrations of the growth of this attitude, which has been influenced by various 'Radical Right' publications. (See Chapter 2 for more details.) However, beyond the glare of the publicity created by the mass media, in schools all over the country there is much valuable teaching and learning taking place, which is putting multi-cultural and anti-racist theories into practice.

While there is a chronological sequence to the development of multi-cultural and anti-racist education, the progress which has taken place is by no means uniform over the whole country. Thus, the education system today contains examples of each of these stages of development within individual LEAs and within individual schools.

Education for ethnic diversity and anti-racist education

We do not intend to define or debate at length the relationship between anti-racist and multi-cultural education. The view taken in this book is that multi-cultural education, or education for ethnic diversity, can stand on its own merits and is also part of the complex whole of anti-racist education.

Education for ethnic diversity in its own right

Britain has for long been and will increasingly be an ethnically diverse society. Children in school now, even if they live at the moment in what is called an 'all-white' area, will inevitably come into contact with people from varied cultures during their lives. Their lives will already be influenced by the reality of our mixed society, through the media and through the changing range of food that they eat, if nothing else. As educationalists, we fail in our aim of preparing children for life if we do not help them towards an understanding and appreciation of the reality of our society as a diverse and changing entity. To encourage children to maintain narrow, rigid, expectations of what is 'normal' and acceptable (which can be the unfortunate end-product of our traditionally ethnocentric education) is to allow them to miss out on the richness, excitement, and beauty of variety which is abundantly available here. It withholds from them the ability to broaden and deepen their expectations of life, for some children possibly permanently.

There is a further dimension to this view of education for ethnic diversity. Nations can no longer easily adopt isolationist attitudes in a world of satellite communications, faster-than-sound travel, and possible nuclear destruction. Peaceful and equitable co-existence depends in some measure on mutual understanding and a willingness to accept variety as normal.

Education for ethnic diversity, within and without our own society, is therefore an essential element which needs to be interwoven into all areas of learning.

Education for ethnic diversity as a part of anti-racist education

Anti-racist education, if it is ever to achieve its aims without bloody revolution, must rely partly upon making people aware of their own prejudices and stereotyped concepts, and upon changing their attitudes. The vast majority of children and adults cannot leap from complete ignorance in this respect to an appreciation of the strangle-hold that institutional racism has on all parts of the life of this country. Most have to come to this realization in stages; multi-cultural education has a part to play in the process.

Education for ethnic diversity strives to widen children's concepts: to enable them to appreciate the essential equality of all people, to accept and value the variations that are possible within broad similarities, to revel in the richness of variety, to recognize stereotyped opinions and to replace them with facts and reason. Such widening is necessary for the shift in perceived reality which is vital if the innate unfairness of racism in all of its forms is to be recognized and then eradicated. Anti-racist education may be ineffective for some people and may antagonize them if multi-cultural education is not also present, encouraging questioning attitudes and constructive thinking in every part of life, and admitting diversity and change as part of the dynamism of life.

These two parts of the complex whole of anti-racist education can work well concurrently. To concentrate on anti-racist education alone is rather like insisting on watching a television programme in black and white when full colour and better comprehension may be achieved with just a small effort in tuning. Conversely, multi-cultural education alone may be likened to watching the programme in colour but with sound and vision hazy and not fully focused.

Use of resources

Negative images

It is important to use all resources with sensitivity and with an awareness of the subtle forms of bias and stereotyping that they can contain. Much of the older material in schools, and even some of the new material that is advertised as multi-cultural, over-emphasizes the negative side of what are sometimes called 'Third World' countries and cultures. It tends to label whole countries as 'under-developed' and to ignore the variety of conditions and cultures within each one. This is akin to looking at a coal-mining village in Wales and inferring, by omission of other information, that that is what the whole of Britain is like. Teachers need to be aware of this feature in materials and should make a positive point of ensuring that the children understand the complexity and variety of conditions in all countries.

Positive images

There are positive points in all people's lives, which will not always be made obvious in the materials that the children use. Teachers will need to emphasize these, to counteract the negative bias which is often present. Examples of this might be the more aesthetic advantages of parts of country life, compared with the more easily recognized material advantages of city life; the closer human relationships of small communities and extended families; the sense of continuity and belonging to be found in long-established villages.

If a child is shown working, positive messages may be given about the satisfaction of helping the family, instead of just the 'poor child' view. The presence of laughter, fun, games, and enjoyment might also not be obvious in some materials and should be included.

Exotic images

To make education for ethnic diversity a normal, integral part of all school life, resources from the varying cultures within and without Britain should be used as any other resources would be. They should be treated not as exotic, to be stared at and remarked on, but as everyday articles of people's lives. Thus, a sari is not a costume but the normal clothing worn by many people both here and in other countries; a wok and chopsticks are simply other people's equivalents of a frying pan and knives and forks; a poster of an Asian bazaar shows just another variation of the world-wide activity of shopping. The more accustomed that the children become to seeing examples of the multiple ways of doing similar activities, the more easily they will view variety as normal and the more readily they will accept that there are usually several ways to reach broadly similar ends.

Bias in materials

Much of the material being used in schools is biased towards a white, middle-class, nuclear family and an often masculine 'norm'. Teachers and children need to be aware of this bias, so that some of its influence may be redressed. Teachers should make a positive point of including in their resources single-parent families, extended families, travelling families, and communal families, instead of devaluing these forms of family life by omission. The material which children see and handle should give equal importance to all of the elements of British society: majority and minority cultures, males and females, working and middle classes, able-bodied and handicapped, young and old. This reflection of Britain must be sensitively portrayed, avoiding patronization and tokenism.

Reviewing materials

Over a period of time, all resources which are used in school should be reviewed to ensure that the multi-cultural nature of British society, and the other aspects mentioned, are properly reflected in them. Many resources will need to be discarded because of the stereotyped and prejudiced views and images that they transmit. Some may be used as teaching points, to illustrate how easily false impressions are conveyed by the visual media. Others may be able to be retained, as long as there are plenty of other good resources around in school to redress the balance.

There are many published check-lists to help teachers to recognize unbiased and balanced materials. Although many are check-lists of books, most of the criteria apply over the range of materials that is used in schools. A few examples are:

Inner London Education Authority (1985) *Everyone Counts*, London: ILEA Learning Resources Branch, 275 Kennington Lane, London SE11 5QZ, tel: 01-735-8202.
This is intended to be about primary mathematics materials but can be applied over the whole range of school areas.
Jones, C. (compiler) (1980) *Assessing Children's Books for a Multi-ethnic Society*, London: ILEA, Learning Resources Branch.
National Union of Teachers (1979) *Guidelines for Teachers on Racial Stereotypes in Textbooks and Learning Materials*, London: National Union of Teachers.
Preiswerk, R. (ed.) (1980) *The Slant of the Pen: Racism in Children's Books*, Geneva: World Council of Churches.
Contains the World Council's own lists for detecting racism in books (regarded by many as the most comprehensive), as well as views from other parts of the world.

Lists of resources, exhibitions, and children's multi-cultural books

Bedfordshire Education Service *LEA (UK) Resources Centres and Contacts: A Teacher's Guide*, Multi-racial Education Resources Centre, c/o Tennyson Road Primary School, Luton LU3 3RS.
Lists the addresses of all of the LEAs in England and Wales, with reference to multi-cultural services where applicable, but does not

detail what is available from them. It is important to obtain the most up-to-date edition, as addresses frequently change.

Centre for Urban Educational Studies (CUES)
Books for Children
Books for Under-Fives in our Multi-Cultural Society
Story Books for Infants and Lower Juniors in the Multi-racial Society
All published by ILEA, Learning Resources Branch, 275 Kennington Lane, London SE11 5QZ, tel: 01-735-8202.

Elkin, J. (Ed.) (1985) *Multi-racial Books for the Classroom*, Library Association, Youth Libraries Group, c/o Central Children's Library, Central Library, Chamberlain Square, Birmingham B3 3HQ.

Elkin, J. (compiler) (1986)
Books for Keeps
Guide to Children's Books for a Multi-Cultural Society
Books for Keeps, 1 Effingham Road, Lee, London SE12 8NZ, tel: 01-852-4953.
Produces guides for ages 0–7 and 8–12.

Evans, R. (1988) *Education in and for a Multi-cultural Society: A Selected Bibliography*.
Rachel Evans is a consultant who mounts exhibitions specializing in curriculum development for equal opportunities in a multi-cultural society. At conferences she can exhibit up to 1500 titles; for colleges, schools, or smaller courses, more specialized exhibitions can be mounted. She also runs workshops, which are appropriate to the course or conference, using the materials to illustrate changes in curriculum strategies. Books may be ordered from Rachel Evans or, in some instances, bought at conferences.
   For further details and costs, Rachel Evans may be contacted by telephone at 0235-23961.

Harmony *Multi-cultural Books for our Children*, Harmony, 22 St Mary's Road, Meare, Glastonbury, Somerset BA6 9SP.

Hessari, R.
   Ruth Hessari has developed a photographic exhibition and various slide presentations which illustrate the practical side of multi-cultural education for primary classes. She has also produced tape/slide training packs for use with teachers and student teachers which are referenced with National Curriculum attainment targets. (These all complement this book.)
   Details may be obtained by phoning 0273-553983.

Klein, G. (1984) *Resources for Multi-cultural Education: An Introduction*, 2nd edn, York: Longman's Resources Unit for SCDC.
This is a valuable source of addresses and information. It contains a section on criteria for selecting classroom material and books, as well as reference to further reading in this area. It lists books on many aspects of multi-cultural education. There is a large section on other resources for teachers: information on and addresses of various organizations and associations, journals, academic centres, projects, in-service courses, LEA resource centres,

bookshops, and audio-visual suppliers. Schools should consider buying a copy, as it contains much information in a concise form, but it is important to obtain the most up-to-date edition because addresses often change. Although it is usually possible to track down an organization or shop through an old address, this can be time-consuming.

Taylor, M. and Hurwitz, K. (1979) *Books for Under-Fives in a Multicultural Society*, London: Islington Library.

2. Multi-cultural education: why, what's going on, and theoretical perspectives

In this chapter, we look first at the evidence which has been amassed to show the need for multi-cultural and anti-racist education. Then we look at the response to that evidence, and to the theorizing about it, by national government, Local Education Authorities, and schools. Next, we discuss the relationships between multi-cultural and anti-racist education. Finally, we study the links between anti-racist, anti-sexist, and anti-classist education and ideology.

The need for multi-cultural and anti-racist education

Evidence of inequality, racism, and racialism

One of the clearest and best presented books within this area is the Runnymede Trust's *Different Worlds: Racism and Discrimination in Britain*, by Gordon and Newnham, which was updated in 1986. This 39-page book contains short chapters on various aspects of racism and discrimination, such as Race and the Law, Housing, Education, the Media. Each chapter has a brief list of further reading. The monthly magazine, *Searchlight*, documents racialist violence, as does *Race Today*. Most Sociology 'A' level and undergraduate textbooks, such as those by Steven Ball, Karen Chapman, and Michael Haralambos, also summarize aspects of racism. Annual Reports from the Commission for Racial Equality (CRE) highlight the deep-rooted nature of discrimination and harassment. A whole series of specialist reports from the CRE (available free of charge) go into graphic and statistical detail; for example, the 1988 Report, *Learning in Terror: A survey of racial harassment in schools and colleges*.

Cecile Wright's in-depth research in two secondary schools of relations and attitudes between white teachers and Afro-Caribbean school pupils, and between white and ethnic minority children, gives verbatim and statistical evidence of stereotyping, under-expectation, and racism. This was published in *Multicultural Teaching* in Autumn 1985. Similar findings are emerging about nursery and primary classes in her 1988–89 research at Leicester University.

In terms of education, by far the most influential text on policymakers and the policy process nationwide has been the Swann Report, *Education for All: The Report of the Committee of Inquiry into the Education of Children from Ethnic Minority Groups*, which was produced, after six years' labour, in 1985. This massive 807-page report, and its subsequent acceptance by all major political parties and Sir Keith Joseph, Conservative Education Minister in 1985, conferred official legitimacy on multi-cultural education.

Four brief summaries of the Report, all under forty pages long, are well worth looking at:

NAME on Swann, published by the National Anti-Racist Movement in Education, is a guide to and critical commentary on the Swann Report. It was produced following disquiet over the official summary sent out by Lord Swann himself.

Swann: A response from the Commission for Racial Equality is not only a valuable and incisive summary of the Report but also a commentary on it.

The Runnymede Trust's *'Education for All': A summary of the Swann Report* is precisely that, a summary.

Education for Equality: The National Union of Teachers' response to the Swann Report is primarily a summary of the Report with brief NUT commentaries.

Each of these four summaries provides a highly valuable starting point for teachers and students wishing to become acquainted with contemporary issues in multi-cultural and anti-racist education. Each summarizes Swann on racism, achievement and underachievement, 'education for all', language and language education, religion and the role of the school, teacher education, the employment of ethnic minority teachers. The first two summaries also give an anti-racist critique of Swann.

At a more theoretical level is *Multi-Racist Britain: New directions in Theory and Practice* by Phil Cohen and Harwant S. Bains.

Pre-dating Swann's publication, though produced while the Committee was sitting, were several useful booklets issued by various teacher trade unions and by local education authorities. Among the most influential and useful are *Our Multi-Cultural Society: The Educational Response*, published by The Assistant Masters and Mistresses Association (AMMA) in 1982; *Education for a Multi-Cultural Society*, the NUT's evidence to the Swann Committee, 1982; the NUT's *Race, Education and Intelligence: A teacher's guide to the facts and issues*, 1982; and three NUT pamphlets, *In Black and White: Guidelines for Teachers on Racial Stereotyping in Textbooks and Learning Materials* (revised in 1982), *Combating Racism in Schools* revised in 1984, and *Prejudice Plus Power: Challenging Racist Assumptions* (1985). Books by authors such as Gillian Klein were also influential; for example her *Reading into Racism: Bias in Children's Literature and Learning Materials* (1985).

LEA and school policies

This material paralleled many excellent documents that were being produced and developed by LEAs. For example ILEA issued a range of booklets such as *Education in a Multi-Ethnic Society: The Primary School* (1984). In 83 pages this booklet puts flesh on the bones of the series of five booklets, *Race, Sex and Class* which were published and widely disseminated in 1983. Booklet 1, *Achievement in Schools*, presents statistical evidence concerning achievement levels of differing ethnic groups in a range of subjects at various ages. Booklet 2, *Multi-Ethnic Education in Schools*, is a tremendously useful 24-page booklet which not only looks at developments in the ILEA schools and education service but also, very importantly, gives a clear and succinct description and critique of three perspectives on ethnic diversity and education. These three perspectives, one emphasizing assimilation, the second emphasizing cultural diversity, and the third emphasizing equality, also comprise the 7-page Booklet 3, *A Policy for Equality: Race*. Booklet 4 in this series is an 8-page whole school policy with very clear guidelines. (Booklet 5 is *Multi-Ethnic Education in Further, Higher and Community Education*.)

ILEA Booklets 3 and 4 are reproduced in Cohen and Cohen's *Multi-Cultural Education: A Source Book for Teachers* (1986), a set of readings on policies and perspectives on the multi-cultural curriculum. One of the most comprehensive policy documents is that produced by the London Borough of Brent. Its *Education for a Multicultural Democracy*, Books 1 and 2, contain a series of questions for schools and teachers on whole school policy, materials and resources, pastoral care, extra curricular activities, primary/nursery education, and each of the school subject areas (for example, 'Is British History restricted to the study of white British people only?'). Such check-lists form part of many LEA documents, for example that of East Sussex, though usually not in such a comprehensive form. Prior to the publication of the Swann Report, a number of other city and county LEAs produced policy documents with implementation and monitoring procedures. Berkshire's *Policy Statement on Racial Equality and Justice* was particularly influential.

James Lynch summarizes well the developments at national and local level up to 1984 in the chapter, 'Policy and Practice', in his *Multi-Cultural Education: Principles and Practice*.

There is no doubt that the legitimizing of multi-cultural (though not explicitly anti-racist) education, by Government acceptance of the Swann Report, spurred on most 'white' LEAs to follow suit. East Sussex LEA, for example, agreed its *Multicultural Education Policy and Support* in 1988, following the Chief Education Officer's attendance at a post-Swann HMI conference, political pressure from the Labour Group of councillors, pressure from some teachers and their unions, and central government funding via educational support grants. Central funding (commitment across the Council Chamber was not sufficient to pay for it out of the rates) was crucial in obtaining all-party support or, in some individual cases, tolerance. When central government funding dried up, the Conservative group voted down the continued personnel funding proposed by the Labour and Democrat groups, though policy and teaching 'modules' continue to be developed and disseminated. The multi-cultural education policy was unanimously adopted in 1988.

Prior to the policy statement, a handful of schools in East Sussex were systematically attempting to make their curricula less ethnocentric. Following the provision of in-service training and of 1.2 full-time equivalent multi-cultural advisory teachers and 0.5 of an advisor, the number of such schools had increased by 1989 but is still only a small fraction of the total. In West Sussex the position is similar. Although there is some involvement in Crawley, the one multi-ethnic town in the county, little is happening elsewhere in terms of developing and putting into practice a whole school curriculum policy.

Implementation at school level is patchy. Chris Gaine's book, *No Problem Here*, includes readable chapters on local authority policies and on developing and achieving a school policy.

An excellent and concise article in the journal *Multicultural Teaching* (1985), by Robin Richardson (Adviser for Multi-Cultural Education for Berkshire at the time of its seminal policy discussions and implementation), looks at factors within and outside schools that affect failure and success in getting a school policy up and running. Chris Gaine's *Getting Equal Opportunities Policies*, does likewise.

The journal *Multicultural Education Review*, published by Birmingham Education Department, is very practical, not only for classroom materials but also in discussing school and LEA policies, their development and difficulties. Most articles are written by school teachers or multi-cultural advisers. The journal *Multiracial Education*, produced by the National Anti-Racist Movement in Education (NAME), has more in-depth analysis of similar issues, usually written by lecturers. Possibly the most useful and widely-read journal, however, is *Multicultural Teaching*, edited by Gillian Klein.

ILEA has published copies of a number of school policies. For example, *Anti-Racist School Policies* was produced by the Multi-Ethnic Inspectorate in 1982. Martin Straker-Welds updated this in 1984 in his *Education for a Multicultural Society: Case Studies in ILEA Schools*. Of course, many hundreds of schools have developed their own policies, with or without LEA stimulus, support, blessing, or directives.

Evaluation of school and LEA response

There is no doubt that, in some schools and LEAs, written policy is virtually dead, which begs the question, 'Multi-cultural Education policies: are they worth the paper they're written on?', the title of a 1983 article by Barry Troyna and Wendy Ball in *The Times Educational Supplement*. This followed revelations that one in three of inner city headteachers actually admitted to ignoring local authority race policies.

For Chris Mullard, Director of the Race Relations Unit at London University's Institute of Education, most anti-racist or multi-cultural education policies 'are rag-bags of good intentions, bits of ideology, strips of anger, and cotton wool balls of love' (quoted by Peter Wilby in the *Independent*, 19 May 1988). However, as teachers are well aware, many schools and some LEAs do not even have a written or considered policy other than (in some cases) an exhortation, without resources or procedures, for implementation and monitoring. According to the 1988 CRE booklet, *Learning in Terror: A survey of racial harassment in schools and colleges*, 77 of the 115 LEAs in England, Wales, and Scotland have multi-cultural/anti-racist policies. Of these, 61 per cent include in their policies, drafts, discussion documents, or working party remits the question of racial harassment of pupils and/or teachers.

By November 1988 (according to John Singh, Senior HMI Staff Inspector, who was speaking at the November 1988 Seminar of ARTEN, the Anti-Racist Teacher Education Network), only 79 out of the 104 LEAs in England and Wales had developed official policies of one kind or another relating to ethnic diversity; 25 had not, despite national legitimation.

A few LEAs wish to soften, modify, or scrap their existing policies. Since the beginning of 1988, a small number of LEAs have indicated their dissatisfaction with anti-racist policies. In 1988, Berkshire discussed the scrapping of its nationally known and seminal policy statement on racial equality and justice which was adopted in 1983. This was commended as a model by the Swann Report and heavily influenced ILEA's *A Policy for Equality: Race*.

A number of Conservative-controlled boroughs, which are at present in the ILEA but which will run their own education services after April 1990, have also indicated their wish to dissociate themselves from ILEA's anti-racist policies.

Berkshire, after a national furore, backed down and kept its policy – for the time being. In describing the move, in *The Times Educational Supplement* in February 1988, Robin Richardson, Adviser for Multi-cultural Education in Berkshire from 1979–85, sets out very strongly and clearly arguments in favour of LEA policy statements. He recognizes that 'policy statements are only pieces of paper, whether at school level or LEA level, and as such they may be totally ineffective and irrelevant. They may in practice be no more than dainty sops to a do-gooding conscience, or frilly sloganizing disguises for inertia and inaction.' However, he continues, 'it is nevertheless the case that formal policy statements have their uses and significance in every important change process, both in schools and LEAs.' They bring issues on to the agenda; they legitimize and encourage developments; they can affect how resources such as officer and in-service time and money are spent; they can affect how syllabus and curricula can be shaped; and they can affect teachers' career and promotion prospects by showing the insights, experience, and commitments that applicants will be expected to have. Richardson concludes that policies 'are not a be-all-and-end-all. But they do have an essential, if humble, role to play.'

The need for this humility concerning policies is apparent from the latest HMI appraisal of schools. Although the situation in primary schools may be different, the most recent, intensive national survey of secondary schools, the 1988 HMI appraisal of secondary schools, suggests that slightly fewer than half of the 185 surveyed secondary schools from 80 LEAs had even considered ways in which the curriculum could contribute to pupils' understanding of multi-ethnic issues. However, the HMI do state that the proportion of schools making such provisions increased between the beginning and end of their survey, which was carried out between 1982–86. Nevertheless, their conclusion is that most schools have yet to come to terms sufficiently in their curricular planning with the fact that their pupils are growing up in a multi-ethnic society.

This was also the conclusion of Bernadette O'Keefe in *Faith, Culture and the Dual System*, comparing Church and County secondary schools. The findings were that only five (13 per cent of) Church school heads who were interviewed saw multi-cultural education as incorporating or requiring a direct engagement with racial discrimination, bias, and stereotyping, and that only 11 per cent of the schools which were studied reported making 'good progress' in developing multi-cultural education. Similar findings are highlighted in Gajendra Verma's *Education for All: a landmark in pluralism*. One survey in the book reveals that forty per cent of a sample of teachers in a largely white area of the North-east insisted that multi-cultural education was not relevant to their schools. Two researchers are quoted in the book as claiming that moving from the metropolitan areas of the Midlands and the North to rural areas of the South-west was like stepping 'on to a new planet'.

The 1988 Education Reform Act and its effects on multi-cultural/anti-racist education

There have been many responses to the Education Reform Act from a variety of multi-culturalist/anti-racist perspectives, in particular to those sections of the Act dealing with religious worship, religious education in the curriculum, opting-out, open enrolment, the National Curriculum, testing, city technology colleges, and the abolition of the ILEA. Examples of such criticisms and commentaries are: publications from the Commission for Racial Equality; current journals in this area of concern, such as 'Multi-cultural Teaching' and 'Issues in Race and Education'; and the pamphlet 'Race Equality and the Education Reform Act' produced by GLARE (Greater London Action for Race Equality).

The section of the Act dealing with religious worship and with religious education is more fully elaborated in the DES circular 3/89 The Education Reform Act (1988): Religious Education and Collective Worship. A change from the 1944 Education Act is that for RE 'new locally agreed syllabuses must reflect the fact that religious traditions in the country are in the main Christian whilst taking account of the teaching and practices of other principal religions'. A further change from 1944, regarding collective worship, is that 'the collective worship in county schools must be wholly or mainly of a broadly Christian character, . . . i.e. most acts of worship in a term must be broadly Christian' (pages 2–3 of the circular). However, the circular continues that 'where it is difficult to reconcile these requirements either in the case of a whole school or of a particular category of pupils', the headteacher can apply for a disapplication for 'the school or any class or description of pupils'. This has been widely criticized in staffrooms as divisive, though in the Circular there is the assertion that 'the

Government believes that all those concerned with religious education should seek to ensure that it promotes respect, understanding and tolerance for those who adhere to different faiths' (page 5 of the circular).

Opting out and open enrolment have been criticized (and also welcomed by a few organizations from various communities) as leading to separatist and ethnically or religiously exclusive schools – as became apparent during and after the 1988 Dewsbury/Kirkless events and the Bradford Muslim Zakaria School application of 1989. The fact that the National Curriculum excludes non-EEC languages such as Russian and Urdu from the foundation subjects has also been criticized.

The National Curriculum Working Party Reports have been criticized by a variety of multi-culturalist and anti-racist writers. It is notable that in the Mathematics and Science National Curriculum documents (the ring folders which were sent to all schools in Spring 1989) the 'cross-curricular issues', such as multi-cultural issues, are not specifically referred to. This is in contrast to the role and place of 'cross curricular themes' such as economic awareness, political and international understanding and environmental education which are specifically detailed in mathematics and science attainment targets and study programmes, see *Science in the National Curriculum* and *Mathematics in the National Curriculum* (DES, 1989).

Some commentators, such as Rehana Minhas writing in *Issues in Race and Education* (Spring 1989), hold the view that 'the National Curriculum is prescriptive, nationalistic, based on ideals of middle-class English chauvinism'. For others, such as Heather Mines writing in the same journal 'there is much that is good and well-informed in the report' – the National Curriculum Council document *English for Ages 5–11* (1988). For her, 'it shows some awareness of the diverse nature of our society'.

Reactions to that same report, produced as paragraph 2.23 of the National Curriculum Council Consultation Report *English 5–11 in the National Curriculum* are similarly mixed:

the positive references made to ethnic and cultural diversity were endorsed, but it was widely felt that its implications could be made more explicit in the programmes of study. It was emphasized that ethnic and cultural diversity should be seen as an enhancement to the quality of education for all children, irrespective of origin. Some respondents noted that no reference was made to gypsies and travellers in the context of ethnic and cultural diversity.

The perspective we take in this book is that whatever legitimation there is for multi-cultural/anti-racist education should be used wherever possible in the schooling system.

Teacher education

What teacher-training institutions are doing about multi-cultural and anti-racist education varies in tone, perspective, extent, and effectiveness but it is undoubtedly more wide-spread in the late 1980s than formerly. Teacher education accreditation bodies such as CATE (Council for the Accreditation of Teacher Education) and the CNAA (Council for National Academic Awards) now insist on a multi-cultural dimension to B.Ed. (Bachelor of Education) and PGCE (Post-Graduate Certificate in Education) courses. In addition, since the assent of these bodies is vital for course approvals and resubmissions, colleges have accordingly changed and improved their courses. Sometimes this is done by including specific courses on 'race and education' or 'multi-cultural education', or by permeating theoretic, practical teaching, and subject study courses with multi-cultural awareness and data. Many courses do both. The days are generally gone when 'education for immigrants' or 'education and ethnic minorities' was taught as part of a 'Special Needs' course. Nevertheless, there is enormous variation between courses.

Such developments (in some cases voluntary, in others obligatory) were stimulated and demanded by, for example, DES Circular 3/84 which laid down, among its criteria for the approval of courses, such prescriptions as: 'Students should be prepared to teach the full range of pupils whom they are likely to encounter in an ordinary school, with their diversity of . . . social background and ethnic and cultural origins. They will need to learn how to respond flexibly to such diversity and to guard against preconceptions based on the race or sex of pupils. . . . They will also need to have a basic understanding of the type of society in which their pupils are growing up, with its cultural and racial mix.' The 1984 CNAA Discussion Paper, *Multi-Cultural Education*, laid down similar criteria for CNAA-validated B.Ed. and PGCE courses.

In 1987, the number of probationer teachers in their first year of teaching who thought that they had been 'very well prepared' or 'quite well prepared' to 'teach children with different cultural backgrounds' was 49 per cent. This showed an increase from the previous survey of probationers by HMI in 1981. However, it is still much less than the 74 per cent who considered that they had been 'very well prepared' or 'quite well prepared' to promote equal opportunities for boys and girls, or the 64 per cent who expressed similar feelings of preparedness for teaching mixed-ability groups. By comparison, only 38 per cent felt similarly prepared for teaching 'socially deprived children'. Thus, the percentage who feel prepared for teaching 'children with different cultural backgrounds' is increasing, but in 1987 was still just under half of the 297 probationers surveyed. This has implications for teachers and student teachers in 'all-white' classrooms and schools. Teachers who are unprepared for teaching children from varied cultural backgrounds are likely to be unprepared for multi-cultural teaching.

It must be added, however, that all but two of those probationers followed B.Ed. and PGCE courses that had been approved by the Secretary of State for Education and Science on the recommendation of CATE. Changes arising from DES Circular 3/84 (also the Welsh Office equivalent, Circular 21/84) and from the establishment of CATE have, since 1984, affected the content and structure of courses as they have come up for validation or revalidation. It is likely that the probationers of 1988 onwards will consider themselves better prepared than their predecessors; by how much may only be guessed at.

What has been done in Colleges and Departments of Education is described and critiqued from an anti-racist perspective by ARTEN, the Anti-Racist Teacher Education Network, in their paper, *Anti-Racist Teacher Education: Permeation: The Road to Nowhere*. Some developments are also described in the journal *Multicultural Teaching*.

What has been done in teacher training is also being criticized by the Radical Right. Michael Trend, writing in the

Spectator in October 1988, criticized various B.Ed. courses at Brighton Polytechnic. Sample criticisms are that 'in the whole of the content of the Multi-Culture course there doesn't appear to be any recognition at all of British culture', and that the courses are typified by 'all the tired old assumptions of the Left, especially those on "anti-sexism" and "anti-racism", dressed in the whole panoply of relativism and social engineering'. Beverley Shaw's chapter, 'Teacher Training: the Misdirection of British Teaching', in Dennis O'Keefe's *The Wayward Curriculum*, attacks teacher education in a similar vein, accusing 'too many teacher trainers' of being 'more interested in radically changing society than in preparing their students for the demanding career ahead of them', of seeing teacher education as a 'collectivist-egalitarian' critique of British society, and of describing the country 'as profoundly unequal and therefore, apparently by definition, unjust. It is described as "institutionally racist".' Shaw criticizes CATE, the Council for the Accreditation of Teacher Education which was set up by Sir Keith Joseph in 1984, for its 'obvious intention . . . to make the study of multi-cultural education a compulsory part of teacher training courses' and bemoans the fact that 'CATE may unwittingly strengthen the strain of utopian, egalitarian and "progressive" thinking in teacher training.'

The Hillgate Group's *Learning to Teach*, Antony O'Hear's *Who Teaches the Teachers?*, and Stuart Sexton's *Our Schools – A Radical Policy* all attack theoretical components of teacher education such as multi-cultural/anti-racist education courses. The first two booklets urge the by-passing of college-based teacher education and its substantial replacement of skills-based learning on-the-job through licensed teacher schemes, or by a two year school-based post-graduate apprenticeship. Both of these schemes received government support in 1988/89. A critique of such developments and the threat to 'reflexive' teacher education is contained in Dave Hill's *The Charge of the Right Brigade: the Radical Right's attack on Teacher Education*.

The inclusion in the National Curriculum of 'gender and multi-cultural issues' as one of the four cross-curricular issues which must be included as part of 'the *whole* curriculum for *all* pupils' (*The National Curriculum: From Policy to Practice* (1989)), may be a countervailing pressure to continue in one form or another courses relating to multi-cultural education, at least for those who do undertake college-based teacher training.

Theoretical relationships between multi-cultural and anti-racist education

In some ways the term 'multi-cultural education', as it is commonly used, is a catch-all phrase which covers a variety of theory and practice.

For some radical anti-racists, the term is more widely acceptable than 'anti-racist education' for a policy, or for Grant Related In-Service Training (GRIST) or for Education Support Grant (ESG), funded by the DES. Such anti-racists adopt the view that, since Conservative governments, LEAs, teachers, and parents are neither willingly nor knowingly going to promote evaluation and analysis of the inegalitarian, classist, racist, and sexist nature of the British power structures, they might as well latch on to a policy that is 'acceptable' to national and local government and redefine/subvert/convert it in the same way that secondary school teachers appear to have redefined the original Conservative government objectives for TVEI (Technical Vocational Educational Initiative).

On the other hand, a number of anti-racists criticize multi-cultural education. Brian Bullivant, for example, in Sohan Modgil's *Multicultural Education: The Interminable Debate*, criticizes much multi-cultural education as having little bearing on children's equality of opportunity and life chances. These, he feels, are influenced more by structural, social class, economic, political, and racist factors, which operate in the wider society, and also by the dominant groups' control over access to social rewards and economic resources. Hatcher and Shallice (quoted in the same book) ask: 'What are we to make of the strange sight of previously recalcitrant and "colour-blind" LEAs now embracing the very principles of multi-culturalism at face value?'

Similar shortcomings in some forms of multi-cultural education are set out in the book edited by Barry Troyna, *Racial Inequality in Education*. Its perspective may be judged from the title (and content) of Ahmed Gurnah's chapter, 'Gatekeepers and Caretakers: Swann, Scarman and the social policy of containment'. Richard Hatcher's chapter, '"Race" and education:

two perspectives for change', extends beyond a critique of multi-culturalism, as set out in the Swann Report (which has virtually nothing to say on systematic racism), and discusses the concern of Giroux and Gramsci with developing 'critical consciousness'.

Writers such as Mike Cole dismiss multi-culturalism, claiming that it does not tackle the real issues of racism and power in society and that it even acts to disguise them by concentrating instead on pluralism and cultural diversity. His chapter in Sohan Modgil's book is an example of this view.

Godfrey Brandt's densely written book, *The Realization of Anti-Racist Teaching*, has a similar perspective but includes (diagramatically) a number of different relationships between multi-culturalism and anti-racism. It seems to us that a four-fold typology of the continuum from multi-culturalism to anti-racism might be useful:

1 Multi-culturalism that ignores and is silent on anti-racism or, indeed, attacks anti-racism,
2 Multi-culturalism that includes anti-racism,
3 Anti-racism that incorporates multi-culturalism,
4 Anti-racism that criticizes multi-culturalism as inadequate and tokenist and that is designed (explicitly or implicitly) as a policy of containing black unrest.

The difference between perspectives 2 and 3 is one of degree; the degree to which institutional and societal racism are made explicit, and the degree of attention paid to them.

Multi-culturalism, even of the 'weak' variety in perspective 1, is under assault from not only some hardline anti-racists on the Hard Left but also the Radical Right, the 'anti-anti-racists' such as Tony Flew, Ray Honeyford, John Marks, Anthony O'Hear, Dennis O'Keefe, Frank Palmer, Roger Scruton, and Alfred Sherman.

The views of the Radical Right are typically set out by Ray Honeyford in a letter to *The Times Educational Supplement* in July 1988:

Britain is not a 'racist society', there is no colour bar in English schools; there is no uniformly depressed and exploited 'black' underclass in this country; and you do not reduce bullying of any kind by setting up committees and appointing anti-racist 'experts'.

In my view, the problem of inter-group conflict in multi-racial schools – which is what most so-called racism actually is – is best tackled in three ways: the establishment of a proper moral education and atmosphere in the school; the exposure of all our children, whatever their background, to that great British cultural tradition which binds us all together; and the rejection of 'anti-racist education' (and the dismantling of the bureaucratic apparatus which supports it).

In Steward Sexton's *GCSE: A Critical Analysis*, the 'nagging anti-racism' of GCSE is attacked. Sherman's chapter attacks GCSE as outlawing national pride and describes its anti-racism as anti-patriotism and an assault on Western Civilization.

Frank Palmer's book, *Anti-Racism: An Assault on Education and Value*, and the chapters by Anthony Flew and John Marks in Dennis O'Keefe's *The Wayward Curriculum*, develop such arguments, which are an attack not only on anti-racism but also on multi-culturalism.

Palmer's book, written from the late 1980s 'radical right' perspective has chapters by Honeyford, Marks, Scruton, and Flew. It is criticized analytically by Julia Neuberger in her 'Hatred as a Moral Virtue: on the latest group diatribe from the anti-anti-racists' in *The Times Educational Supplement*, December 1986. From a liberal, multi-cultural perspective, she attacks both the Radical Right and some aspects of the anti-racists' views. In this she is not alone.

Perspectives 3 and 4 are also under attack from some liberal writers such as Jeffcoate, who, for example in *Ethnic Minorities and Education*, attacks ILEA as illiberal in its anti-racist policies. Jeffcoate is described by Chris Gaine, in *No Problem Here*, as 'part of a backlash against the kind of anti-racism supported in this [Chris Gaine's] book'.

This liberal critique is apparent also in books such as Maurice Craft's *Education and Cultural Pluralism*, which is rooted in a cultural diversity/'weak multi-cultural' tradition.

It must be added that a number of highly useful books deliberately avoid offering a particular perspective; for example, Twitchin and Demuth's *Multi-Cultural Education: Views from the Classroom*, which is very practical and is based firmly on what happens in schools, and Nixon's *A Teacher's Guide to Multicultural Education*.

While we accept that some of the anti-racists' criticisms are valid for some of the practice carried out in schools, their view is not our view as it is expressed here and in Chapter 1. Unlike some anti-racists, we do not criticize multi-culturalism as being inherently tokenist and incapable of leading towards anti-racism. While not totally dismissing 'vanguardism' (the setting out and extending of analyses and programmes which are in advance of those views held in common contemporary consciousness), it seems to us that such a purist view, which demands a great leap in development for many teachers and students, serves to exclude many teaching professionals from participating in the attack on racism. (A parallel might be the manner in which some socialist sects exclude potential recruits to socialism by their insistence on ideological, political, and organizational purity and on separatism from more mainstream, and more numerous, allies.) This is not to deny that today's 'vanguardism' or avant-garde may become tomorrow's common sense.

It is also obvious that we reject the views of the Radical Right 'anti-anti-racists'. Similarly, we have no time for the standpoint of those liberal critics who oppose any anti-racism. We agree that some anti-racist LEA behaviour and Racism Awareness Training has been crude, authoritarian, and grossly mismanaged. The *Macdonald Inquiry into Racial Violence in Manchester Schools*, which followed the racist murder of 13-year old Ahmed Iqbal Ullah at Burnage High School for Boys, attacks the crudeness of what it calls 'moral anti-racism' which stigmatizes all whites, and sets out its support for more sensitive anti-racism, with examples of good practice. The perspective in this book is that anti-racism must include (and supplement) multi-culturalism, and that multi-culturalism should lead on to an anti-racist understanding and action.

Anti-racism, anti-sexism, anti-classism

In this book we do not set out to present a critique of the theoretical analysis of society, schooling, and race that is necessary for understanding why we should encourage multicultural learning and teaching. However, the following books, policies, and writings should help to develop such an understanding, and also a greater understanding of the inter-relationship between anti-sexism, anti-classism, and anti-racism and multi-culturalism.

A concern for and commitment to anti-racism is linked in the minds of some teachers and students with critiques that designate society and schools as sexist and classist as well as racist. Such a Marxist perspective suggests that schools repro-duce the existing social class pattern and thus reproduce and amplify existing social inequalities: most working-class children go into working-class jobs and relative powerlessness, most middle-class children go into middle-class jobs, and most upper-class children go, via private schools, into the upper-class power elite. Most 'A' level and undergraduate Sociology textbooks summarize such arguments. For example, those by Michael Haralambos, Steven Ball, and Karen Chapman very clearly summarize and explain Marxist, liberal democratic, and conservative structural-functionalist concepts of the linkages between schooling and society and between schooling and race.

Chris Gaine's book, *No Problem Here: A Practical Approach to Education and 'Race' in White Schools*, contains an easily read, 12-page final chapter linking 'race' inequality with inequalities of class, sex, and also disability.

Another book, which is easy to read but more detailed, is Madan Sarup's, *The Politics of Multiracial Education*. This book discusses and critiques multi-racial education, racism, and education. It also discusses the relationships between hegemony (the way in which the views, attitudes, and values of one class dominate in a society and become that society's 'common sense') and race, class, and gender, and criticizes a number of approaches that stress cultural pluralism. Sarup's ideas are also developed in his earlier, more general book, *Education, State and Crisis: A Marxist Perspective*.

A seminal book, which is, however, far more difficult to read but which is at the forefront of contemporary updating of radical and Marxist analyses of education, is Henry Giroux's *Theory and Resistance in Education: A Pedagogy for the Opposition*. This compelling book applies Gramscian concepts to radical pedagogy (pedagogy being the pattern of pupil-teacher inter-action, learning, and teaching). Some of these concepts are more simply and more generally set out in Roger Simon's *Gramsci's Political Thought: An Introduction*. Giroux's critique is further developed in his *Education Under Seige*.

One radical local education authority, ILEA, has investigated and published evidence on and policies concerning this trilogy of interconnected inequalities. Possibly alone of the 104 LEAs in England and Wales, ILEA has published major reports on all three aspects, focusing on the need to value major aspects of all cultures, not just the dominant white, male, middle-class culture. Of course, tens of thousands of teachers and thousands of schools try to do the same. The ILEA booklet *Race, Sex and Class 1: Achievement in Schools*, already referred to, sets out extremely clearly data on social class, sex, and ethnic differences in educational attainment and, for each type of inequality, summarizes very briefly theories about why these differences exist and what has been done, evaluates how successful these initiatives have been, and suggests what else could be done – all in 23 pages, with 158 references!

Both of Mike Cole's 1989 books, *The Social Contexts of Schooling* and *Education for Equality: Some Guidelines for Good Practice*, set out relationships between anti-racism, anti-sexism, and anti-classism. The first is more theoretical and has a comparative international dimension. The second, while rooted in theory, includes chapters on nursery education, infant schooling, and junior schooling. There are also some schools which have developed or are in the process of developing school policies on race, gender, and class.

We believe that anti-racism and multi-culturalism can lead to and be informed by anti-classism and anti-sexism. Many teachers substitute the word and concept 'class' (or 'sex') for 'race' in check-lists for stereotyping, policies concerning equal opportunities, appointments policies, classroom activity choices or subject option choices in secondary schools.

It is an enlightening experience to look, for example, at an anti-racist or multi-cultural check-list for stereotyping in books and to replace the word 'race', wherever it occurs, with the word 'class'. Similarly, just as it is possible to look at the different amount of time and types of response given by teachers to boys and girls in the same class, it is interesting to look at how working-class and middle-class children are treated differently. Carol Adams' *Implementing the ILEA's anti-sexist policy: a guide for schools* could very profitably be used with reference to race and class as well as to sex discrimination, as could many LEA anti-sexist policies, such as Devon's.

Again, while there is considerable literature on and research into British Asian children being steered towards maths and sciences, and British Afro-Caribbean children being channelled into music and sports activities in secondary school option choice and in primary classroom activities, there is a difference in policy reaction between ethnic group stereotyping and teacher expectation on the one hand, and social class stereotyping and teacher expectation on the other. That is to say, the dangers of 'race' stereotyping are clearly spelt out in hundreds of policies but there are very few such policies regarding social class stereotyping.

It is true that there is a whole body of literature on social class stereotyping and social class reproduction. (For example, books by Willis, Corrigan, Bowles and Gintis, and Giroux are all usually referred to in standard up-to-date sociology of education readers.) However, while research is translated into some national, LEA, and school policies concerning 'race', research has steadfastly *not* been turned into policy as far as class is concerned, beyond a small handful of 'Radical Left' city areas. Both the ILEA Thomas and Hargreaves Reports stand virtually in isolation in trying to do for 'class' what very many LEAs are trying to do for race. These two reports, *Improving Primary Schools* (the 'Thomas Report' of 1985) and *Improving Secondary Schools* (the 'Hargreaves Report' of 1984) were both explicitly addressing the underachievement of working-class pupils and developing policies to raise the achievement levels (defined in a number of ways) of such pupils.

Many teachers (and indeed the Thomas and Hargreaves Reports) see the connections between the ways in which the formal curriculum and the hidden curriculum and pedagogy can be used to empower children and all types of communities instead of (however unintentionally) systematically degrading and demeaning them. However, the day is not yet near when a government will set up a Commission for Class Equality or will empower the Equal Opportunities Commission to deal with cases of social class discrimination. Other than the two ILEA reports into improving the educational and life chances of working-class pupils, there has been little in the way of practical policy proposals, applying the gamut of egalitarian theory, beyond 'comprehensivizing' and 'spending more on'. The Labour Party, throughout its local government conferences in the eighties and the setting out of its national policies, seems to have become stuck in the groove of arguing for more resources, more comprehensivizing, and more equal opportunities for ethnic minorities and for females, and of reacting to the divisive, elitist, and anti-egalitarian thrust of Conservative education legislation.

One notable exception is the article, 'A Socialist Education Policy', by Caroline Benn and the STA (Socialist Teachers Alliance), in which a number of detailed proposals are set out. (This can be found as an appendix in Cole's book, *The Social Contexts of Schooling*.) Other exceptions are to be found in the practice of probably hundreds of schools – in their curricular materials, pedagogies, and hidden curricula, and in their relationships between pupils and teachers, and between teachers, schools, and local communities. It remains true, however, that developments in anti-sexism, anti-racism, and 'anti-classism' are treated and disseminated very differently by national and local government and in schools, yet they can, and should, learn from each other.

Use of this book

The ideas in this book will be used by readers with a great variety of experiences and view points. Some, from religious or ethical beliefs, will stress liberalism and tolerance. Some will react to first or second-hand racial and/or social injustice. Some will adopt a 'meritocratic' concern when any social group is perceived to be underachieving and disabled in joining society's pool of talent. Some will worry about inner city rebellions, the threat to the *status quo*, and the threat to social and economic stability caused by ethnic minority alienation. Some will accept a Marxist analysis of the relationship between schooling and society, of the relationship between race, gender, and class inequality, of the role of schools as part of the 'ideological state apparatus' in legitimizing and perpetuating this inequality. Last but not least, some will be 'doing multi-culturalism' because they have been told to do so.

This book may be used by all of those. The teacher or student teacher who is new to multi-culturalism, who is hesitant and anxious about it, will find this book a very easy and accessible entry point.

We do hope that it will be a take-off point in developing an individual or (better) a collaborative anti-racist perspective. We hope that anti-racist policies at national, LEA, school, and classroom levels will be more effectively developed, implemented, monitored, and evaluated instead of being, in some cases, merely the rhetorical flavour of the month. With the advent of the National Curriculum in primary schools, we must ensure that anti-racism and multi-culturalism do not become the flavour of *last* month.

Our perspective is identical to that expressed by Gerry German, Principal Education Officer of the Commission for Racial Equality, in the *Times Education Supplement* in July 1988:

Multi-cultural policies go part of the way to promote understanding and respect. Anti-racist policies set about countering the combination of individual attitudes and institutional practices that are based on ingrained ideas of black inferiority and white superiority and which exclude ethnic minority children from the full range of opportunities to which they are entitled – and which limit the intellectual and emotional development of white children, too.

Real education is about meeting children's needs and developing their potential.

It is about promoting self-confidence, respect and co-operation. It is about learning from the wisdom of the whole of humanity rather than confining experience to mono-lingual, mono-cultural nation frontiers. Multi-culturalism opens the mind to the whole world as do world and development studies. Racism is about discord, inequality and injustice – and anti-racism is about the education strategies that schools need to adopt if all children are to be given a real education and a chance to succeed rather than fail.

In many schools, the development and collaborative implementation of multi-cultural/anti-racist policies has considerably altered not only school policy and pedagogy but also the teachers. We have taught, researched, or observed in schools in East Sussex, West Sussex, Nottinghamshire, and Inner London. Not only in the many multi-ethnic schools but also in the all-white schools, we have seen that teachers' and children's knowledge, attitudes, understanding, and evaluation have changed. They must continue to do so: this is the challenge for present and future teachers.

Part II Practical ideas for the primary classroom

3. The National Curriculum

The National Curriculum clearly recognizes the necessity of multi-cultural education within the curriculum for *all* children, and the value of topic work both to deliver multi-cultural education and to achieve the attainment targets expected of primary age children (*The National Curriculum: From Policy to Practice*: 1989, para. 3.8, 4.3, 4.8).

Teachers and student-teachers can and should become very efficient in using the wide breadth of multi-cultural education to add substance to the bare bones of all the attainment targets of the National Curriculum subjects; the attainment targets (abbreviated to ATs) of the core subjects of the National Curriculum, English, Mathematics and Science, are looked at below, in relation to the areas covered in Part II of this book.

English

The methods of working which are suggested throughout Part II are well suited to the achievement of AT1, Speaking and Listening, at all the primary levels. Through the use of these methods, the children can gradually develop the skills and abilities which enable them to listen attentively; to contribute and respond to discussions; to debate, describe, explain, relate and retell; to express opinions; to ask and answer questions. Aspect 5, Thinking and questioning in Chapter 5 is particularly relevant here. AT1 requires children to be actively aware of accents, dialects and other languages. Ways of achieving this awareness feature in many of the Themes (particularly Communications), and in many of the Aspects and Strands, (particularly Strand 1, Language Diversity).

AT2, Reading, is equally fully covered through the work described in Part II. Children will find material to sustain their interest in reading while they acquire the skills necessary to become fluent, accurate readers. The range of stories, poems and rhymes which is implicit in multi-cultural work give the children the greatest possible scope in which to experience the many styles in which they are written. The multi-cultural Themes, Aspects and Strands actively encourage the gradual development of skills which help the children to make effective use of information and reference sources, and to put what they 'infer, deduce, predict, compare and evaluate', (level 5), to effective use in discussion.

The work we suggest will provide interesting and varied material to sustain the gradual development of the writing skills detailed in AT3. It gives unlimited opportunity for children to write for the purposes and in the styles indicated in this AT, for instance, to 'write stories' (level 2), to 'write in other forms than narrative', and 'produce independently longer pieces of writing' (level 3), and to 'organize non-chronological writing in a logical way' (level 4). The areas of work and development covered in the five aspects for personal and social development (Chapter 5) are very relevant to the gradual achievement of the final point made in level 5, to 'write accounts of personal experiences, or poems, that reveal the engagement of the writer's personal feelings.'

AT4, Spelling, and AT5, Handwriting, can both be achieved through all of the multi-cultural work suggested here.

Mathematics

The multi-cultural material available to the children within the work described here, and other similar work, provides a vast range of data which they can utilize to gain experience in ATs 1 and 9, Using and Applying Mathematics, the Number ATs 2–5, and the Data Handling ATs 12–14. For example, in Food topics children can work with various sets of fruits which originate in several countries, but are available here, to help gain an understanding of the conservation of number (AT2).

Many of the manipulations of number detailed in AT3 can be practised using multi-cultural source material, for instance, in Home topics children could work out how many people must share a bedroom when families of varying sizes live in houses with a set number of rooms available. In Journey topics, the length of time taken for particular journeys, using various means of transport, can be estimated (AT4). Children can collect, record, process and interpret data, (ATs 12 and 13), from Communication topics. For instance, they could study how many languages they know about or how many people speak different languages in Britain, making use of mapping diagrams, block and line graphs, bar and pie charts, frequency tables, pictograms and so on. Teachers will be able to pitch the level of work to suit the development of the children, and to find enough variety within it to sustain their interest as they gain the necessary experience of the various processes and procedures detailed in these attainment targets.

Areas covered in AT8, Measures, are important aspects of many of the Themes, for example, using suitable measures for time in Celebration topics, for distances in Journey topics, for weighing in Food topics, and so on. They are also applicable to much that is covered in the five aspects for personal and social development, for example, various measurements in Self-awareness, and Awareness of others, also in Strand 2, Ethnic diversity within Maths.

Many of the areas covered in AT10, Recognizing and Using the Properties of Two- and Three-dimensional Shapes, are given concrete meaning when used in the context of the multi-cultural work illustrated here, which also gives teachers the widest possible range for showing the practical application of shape in real life. For example, finding and using shapes with which to decorate hats in the patterns from many cultures in a Hat topic; finding the shapes used in the variety of homes in which people live, in Shelter topics; discovering how shapes are used in the packaging for many foods, in a Food topic, and so on.

Real-life situations to illustrate much of AT11, Recognizing Location and using Transformations in the Study of Space, are also easily drawn from the suggestions for work given here. For example, compass work drawn from Journey topics, and work using symmetry drawn from the use of patterns within several of the themes.

Science

Much of the material used in and generated by multi-cultural topics of all kinds will be suitable for investigating and recording by the methods mentioned in AT1, the Exploration of Science.

Multi-cultural education is grounded in the similarities and variations within and between human life, and the intimate connections that human life has with all else on Earth. It is not surprising, therefore, that AT2, The Variety of Life, AT3, Processes of Life, and AT4, Genetics and Evolution, contain references which relate to points from almost all of the Themes, the five personal and social development aspects, especially to Aspects 2 and 3, Self-awareness and Awareness of others, and the three interweaving strands, in particular Strand 3, Ethnic diversity around school. Food topics are particularly relevant to AT3, which refers to diet, malnutrition, good health and so on.

AT5, Human influences on the Earth, contains many points about pollution and waste products which can be examined and debated in topics such as Shelter. Some of the areas contained in this attainment target will provide interesting material with which to extend work on Aspect 4, Relationships, for example to 'know that human activity may produce local changes on the Earth's surface, air and water' (level 3).

Multi-cultural topics will be useful mediums in which to pin down the practicalities of some of the learning required in AT6, Types and Uses of Materials, and AT7, Making New Materials. For example, knowing which materials, natural and man-made, are suitable for which purposes through the experience of handling and seeing many objects from many cultures; and knowing that raw materials from many countries are needed for manufacturing processes.

Parts of AT9, Earth and Atmosphere, likewise become meaningful when examples are drawn from topics such as Shelter ('know that the weather has a powerful effect on people's lives') and Food ('know that climate determines the success of agriculture and understand the impact of occasional catastrophic events').

Journey topics will provide practical examples for some of the areas contained in AT10, Forces, helping children 'understand that pushes and pulls can make things start moving, speed up, swerve or stop', and 'understand that the movement of an object depends on the size and direction of the forces exerted on it', for example. Home topics will relate to parts of AT11, Electricity and Magnetism; Communication topics to parts of AT12, Information Technology; Journey, Food, Shelter and Home topics to some of AT13, Energy; Celebration topics to areas of AT14, Sound and Music, AT15, Light, and AT16, The Earth in Space (seasons, etc.). AT17, The Nature of Science, at level 4 (scientific advance) is relevant to historical aspects of several of the Themes.

These examples show only a few of the connections between the work described here and the National Curriculum attainment targets. There are many more which occur quite naturally within multi-cultural education. Teachers will find that the enormous range of work and material made available to them through multi-cultural education will enable them to fulfil the requirements of the National Curriculum in an interesting and relevant manner.

Figure 1 Main topic web, 'Ourselves', highlighting Themes 1–7 and Aspects 1–5 discussed in this book

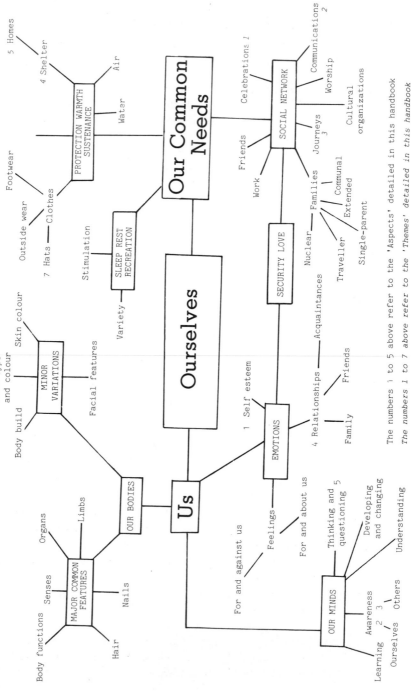

The numbers 1 to 5 above refer to the 'Aspects' detailed in this handbook

The numbers 1 to 7 above refer to the 'Themes' detailed in this handbook

4. Seven themes for ethnically diverse topics

Introduction

The seven themes detailed in this chapter come from the Common Needs part of the topic web entitled 'Ourselves'. They have been chosen at random to illustrate how topics which are often used in schools can be permeated with multi-cultural features. It is hoped that they illustrate some of the ways that the skills, concepts, and attitudes mentioned earlier may be introduced to, and developed with, the children. They aim to widen children's horizons and to set the work that they do at school into a world-wide context.

Each theme starts with a topic web to spark off individual teachers' ideas for work that their class could do. The main topic webs are not meant to represent a rigid plan of work but merely show areas that could be covered.

A brief list, Teacher aims, concentrates on emphasizing the universality of the themes and the fascinating variety within the overall, essentially common elements. The ability to integrate all subjects into each topic is pointed out.

The list, Pupil objectives, concerns areas which the children may be able to cover, depending on exactly what each teacher includes in the scope of the topic. Many of the separate items here could form the basis of a complete piece of work for a class.

The Subject breakdowns are intended to provide starting points for the content of the themes and to replace the usual concentration on traditional material with a broader mix of

Figure 2 Sample topic web, 'Celebrations'

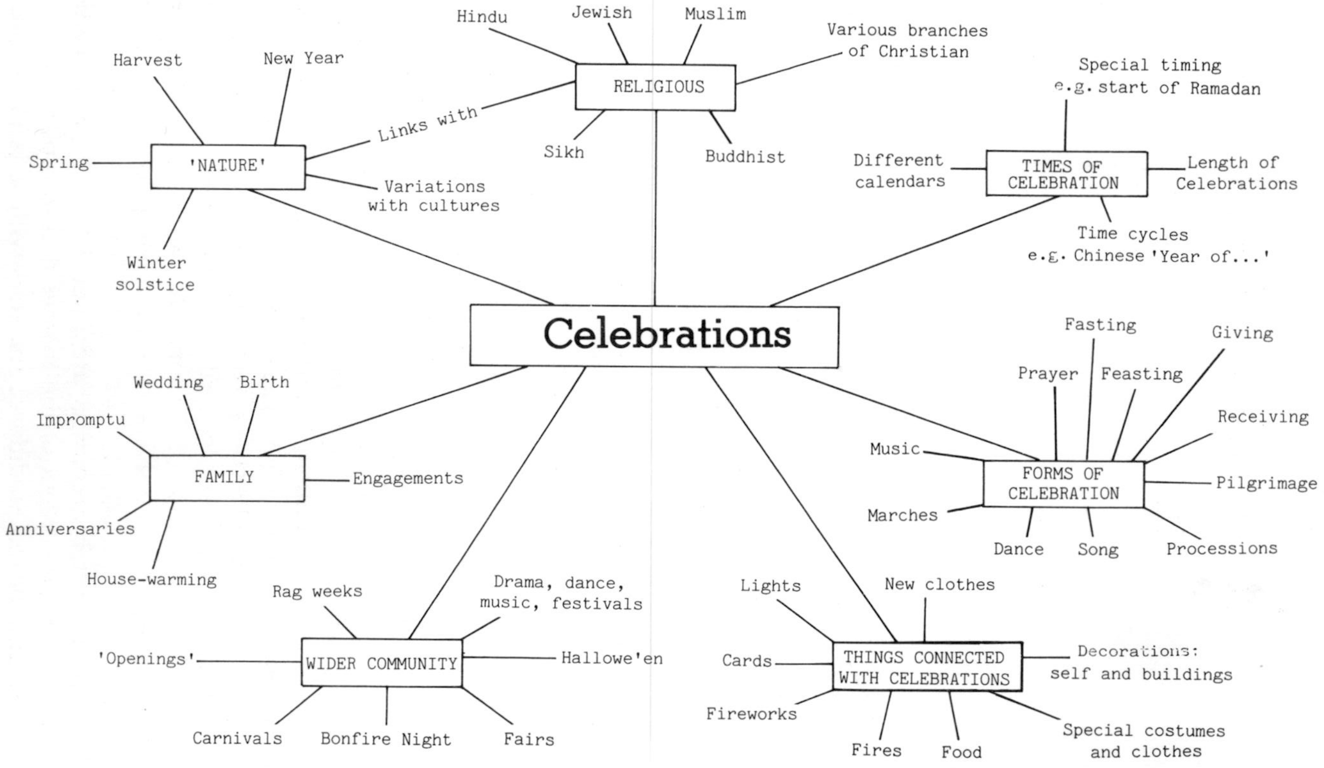

influences. Much emphasis is placed throughout on including the diversity of modern Britain in all areas, by illustrating *all* parts, not just the obvious 'other culture' parts, with ethnically mixed illustrations and examples. This is so important for making ethnic diversity a normal part of school.

The list of Resources is intended to provide ideas and suggestions which teachers can develop for their own situations. Many of the same publications are included in several themes. This is deliberate, as we recognize that schools do not have unlimited supplies of books available, that books which are bought need to be versatile, and that it is preferable for the multi-cultural books to be permanently in school and not just available on loan. Many of the children's books featured are to be found in schools and may be used as resources for many topics. For example, *Pavan is a Sikh* by Sean Lyle may be used as a resource for celebrations, hats, language, and food, as well as for themes that are not illustrated here.

Some of the themes also contain supplementary topic webs. These have been included to give examples of how part of a complex idea can be used as a feasible basis for a piece of work.

Theme 1: Celebrations

Celebrations is a topic that is often used in schools and is often chosen as a suitable vehicle for the first foray into multi-cultural work. Pitfalls, such as tokenism, can be avoided by looking at the universality of celebrations – all the similarities within what is celebrated and how it is celebrated – rather than by concentrating on strange and colourful scenes from which the fundamental elements are not drawn out or discovered by the children. Thus, many celebrations for harvest or spring could be investigated, to discover the similarities, and the variations within these similarities. The use of cards for celebrations, looked at across many cultures, would place the topic firmly on a basic similarity; the variations within cards could be appreciated by the children from a familiar starting point. Other commonalities of celebrations – food, music, decorations, rituals – could be handled in the same way.

Celebration could form a small part of a larger topic: for example, looking at visits and journeys connected with celebrations as part of a topic on Travelling or Journeys, or looking at significant dates for celebrations in a Time or Seasons topic.

Celebrating sad occasions should be included and connections should be made, within Celebrations topics of all sorts, with these times. Thus, the rituals of commemorating tragedies, the clothes worn to funerals, national remembrances, and so on, across many cultures, have a part to play.

The cultural mix of modern British society can be shown by using varied illustrations for our 'traditional' occasions, by including (in collages and friezes) people with authentic skin tones, faces, hairstyles, and clothes; by choosing stories with British people from black, Asian, and other minority cultures as central characters, especially when these are 'ordinary' stories; and so on. The scope and possibilities within Celebration topics are endless. Once the area is considered from the standpoint of ethnic diversity, teachers will find many ways of creating work which both broaden the children's outlook and are tailored to their own particular situations.

Teacher aims

* To show the many similarities in the ways in which people celebrate across various cultures,
* To incorporate work from most subject areas into the topic.

Pupil objectives

* To enable the children to understand and appreciate:

WHY people celebrate
— to unify a society, to keep up links with each other,
— to give society a meaning and a timescale,
— to maintain traditions and customs; for continuity,
— to help people to maintain arduous lifestyles,
— to provide a break from routine,
— to mark stages through life,
— for reasons of faith and religion; beliefs,
— because they like to, for exuberance, joyfulness.

WHEN they celebrate
— at significant times in human life: birth, death, marriage,

coming of age,
— at significant times of the natural year: midwinter, new year, spring, harvest (across various cultures),
— at significant times of the various religious calendars: Eid, Ramadan, Easter, Channukah, Diwali,
— for varying lengths of time: Sabbath, birthdays – one day; Chinese New Year, Carnival – several days,
— at different times for similar occasions: different times of New Year, moving patterns of Easter, Ramadan, Chinese New Year, etc.

WHAT they celebrate
— any event, happening, season, natural phenomena, occurrence, or occasion that is significant to them.

WHERE they celebrate
— religious buildings: temple, church, synagogue, sikh gurdwana, etc.,
— homes: family celebrations; some religious occasions,
— meeting halls: religious and family celebrations, community celebrations,
— open air: carnival, funeral, fireworks, processions.

HOW they celebrate
— giving: cards, presents, alms, greetings, thought,
— receiving,
— wearing new clothes,
— special foods,
— fasting,
— decorating homes, buildings,
— decorating selves: masks, hand and foot painting, costumes, jewellery, etc.,
— family gatherings, visits, journeys,
— processions,
— prayer,
— light: candles, lanterns, divas, fairy lights, fireworks,
— music and drama.

Celebrations: a breakdown through curriculum subject areas

Reading, and writing

Reading and writing are involved at many levels in all aspects of Celebration topics and both activities may be tailored, within areas of the particular topic, to suit individual children's immediate and longer-term needs. Thus, a child who needs stretching in her/his reading can be directed towards fairly taxing reading material, while one who needs the confidence of success can work with material well within her/his scope.

Poetry, rhymes, and story

The choice here is endless and will include many favourites of both children and teacher. Small elements within poems, rhymes, and stories may be given new significance by the slant of the particular topic: for example, noticing the 'giving' aspect in a story which incidentally contains a birthday, or noticing the food mentioned in passing which links with celebratory food.

There is a wide selection of books available which feature various aspects of celebrations from the viewpoint of British black and Asian people; some books can be found with British people of many cultures involved in traditional British celebrations.

Children can be encouraged to discover the origins of fairytales which often form the basis of pantomimes – a traditional part of Christmas – and to compare the similarities which occur between tales from many cultures.

Language

Children can be encouraged to look at words for celebrations in a variety of languages and scripts. Collecting descriptive words about parts of the topic could lead on to using them creatively, perhaps through dance and movement as a change from writing. The children could be encouraged to project themselves into other people's experiences by using words to describe imagined emotions about celebrations. They could investigate words connected with celebrations which we have borrowed from other languages.

Maths

Calendars (and the special days on them) and time cycles

could be studied within this topic area, as could the way in which certain religious timings are calculated. Times and dates could be written in various number scripts. The timing of processes for preparing and cooking celebratory food could be included, as could weighing.

Measuring, shape, pattern, and symmetry are involved in decorations of many sorts, including face and body painting, and hand and foot decoration. Money is involved in costing items, and activities such as comparing postage costs could be looked at.

Sets, graphs and charts can be drawn from many aspects of Celebration topics: how many celebrations do these religions have each year? when does harvest start in these countries? sets of birthday candles, and so on.

Science

Human science (birth, growth, and death) and natural science (from planting to harvest and utilization or decay) form part of some Celebration topics. Aspects of social science might be included: how and why celebrations change according to the numbers of people present, why humans need to celebrate, what part celebrations play in social control, and so on.

Aspects of light could be investigated, as could the properties of light-giving materials such as wax, oils, gas, electricity, and gunpowder, and the forms that celebratory lights can take.

Studies could be made of fasting and feasting and their effects on us, and the use and mis-use of alcohol and drugs at times of celebrations.

Geography

Children could discover the countries of origin of some of the many celebrations seen in this country. They could find out where some of our traditional artefacts come from: Christmas trees, simnel cakes, and so on. They could see if there is a geographic significance for any celebrations, and could work out how geographic position affects some celebrations: when is harvest in New Zealand? what is Christmas like on the beach in Australia? They could try to discover whether foods (e.g. pumpkin pie, sweet red rice) or clothes are used in some celebrations because of geographic influence.

History

Most celebrations are traditional in one way or another within families and/or within cultures. Children could look into their own lives to find celebrations or aspects of them which are particular to them. They could make personal or family 'life-lines', marked with the causes for all forms of celebrations, including mourning and remembrance.

The historic reasons for some of the celebrations that take place in Britain could be investigated: the spread of Christianity, the mingling of Pagan and Christian rites, the ways in which immigration over the ages has introduced new traditions of celebration.

The basic human need to mark occurrences, and the similarities of methods across cultures and historic ages, could also be studied.

R.E.

The celebrations within various faiths could be, or form part of, a complete topic. The fundamental similarities between these celebrations could be looked at, as could the forms of expression that these similarities take: the common use of prayer, music, fasting, feasting, giving. The religious significance of particular aspects of celebrations could be included within wider topics.

Artwork

Children can illustrate most areas of these topics with artwork, using influences from many cultures, and can also use art forms as a means to express themselves. They can make cards, masks, lanterns, decorations, clothes, wall pictures, and may perhaps look at one particular area across several British cultures. Traditional shapes of, and decorations for, celebratory food would be an interesting area for artwork; the children could create their own in paints and glue, etc. Celebratory symbols could be drawn; the children could use their imaginations to create some that have particular meaning for them, as individuals.

Music

Children may listen to music associated with various celebrations and sing songs from them. Perhaps certain instruments are connected with a particular celebration (e.g. marching bands for religious groups, steel bands for Carnival) or perhaps an instrument is used throughout several (e.g. bells for weddings, funerals, church services, New Year, spreading news).

Music and song form one of the common elements in many forms of celebration across many cultures.

Dance, movement, and drama

All three areas may be used creatively to express aspects of celebrations: enjoyment, happiness, sorrow, giving, receiving, thoughtfulness, reflection, remembrance.

Particular forms of dance, movement, and drama are associated with certain celebrations: Maypole dancing, Morris dancing, the drama of Rama and Sita, the Passion plays. Children can be encouraged to discover the universality of these in human celebrations.

Celebrations: some resources

Resources from the children

Children can contribute their own memories of celebrations; photographs of family celebrations; pictures of celebrations from other cultures; cards, decorations, special clothes and jewellery; articles that they associate with certain celebrations; materials to make their own class 'Celebration'.

Resources in the local and wider community

There might be children and/or staff within the school who are willing to describe celebrations from their particular culture and how they actually celebrate them in Britain.

Parents and other people from the local minority communities might be willing to show the children how they celebrate in this country (rather than show how it is done in the original country of origin), with the aim of emphasizing the here and now instead of something 'out there'/'somewhere else'/'far away'.

There may be religious buildings of several faiths that can be visited; likewise, shops which supply articles for celebrations.

Television now often shows the celebration of major festivals in this country, such as Chinese New Year, and Carnival.

Published resources

Children's books

(*Containing references to and information about the areas indicated*)
Bennett, O. (1984) *Kikar's Drum*, London: Hamish Hamilton.
   Hindu festival of Raksha Bandhan; Sikh wedding preparations.
Bennett, O. (1985) *A Sikh Wedding*, London: Hamish Hamilton.
   Preparation for and celebration of a wedding.
Blakely, M. (1977) *Nahda's Family*, London: A. & C. Black.
   Eid and Ramadan.
Cornell, J. (1981) *Sharing Nature With Children*, London: Exley Publications.
   For Science aspects.
Ganly, H. (1986) *Jyoti's Journey*, London: Andre Deutsch.
   A picture story-book, with an Indian wedding.
Harlen, W. (1985) *Primary Science: Taking the Plunge*, London: Heinemann Educational.
   For Science aspects.
Knapp, C. (1979) *Shimon, Leah and Benjamin*, London: A. & C. Black.
   Jewish celebrations: Bar Mitzvah, Passover, Purim, Sabbath.
Lawton, C. (1984) *Matzo and Bitter Herbs*, London: Hamish Hamilton.
   Passover: preparations for, customs of; seder: passover food.
Lyle, S. (1977) *Pavan is a Sikh*, London: A. & C. Black.
   Sikh festivals.
McCarty, N. (1977) *Rebecca is a Cypriot*, London: A. & C. Black.
   Greek orthodox wedding.
Solomon, J. (n.d.) *Bobbie's New Year*, London: Hamish Hamilton.
   Sikh celebrations; Baisakhi Festival.
Solomon, J. (1980) *Gifts and Almonds*, London: Hamish Hamilton.
   Muslim celebrations for Eid and Ramadan.
Solomon, J. (1984) *Sweet Tooth Sumil*, London: Hamish Hamilton.
   Hindu festival of Diwali (Festival of Light).
Steele, P. (1983) *Festivals around the World*, London: Macmillan Children's Books.
   Library. Large, colourful pictures.

Tsow, M. (1982) *A Day with Ling*, London: Hamish Hamilton.
References to Chinese New Year.
Festivals, London/Basingstoke: Commonwealth Institute/Macmillan Education.
Looks at Ramadan, Eid-ul-Fitr, Carnival, Diwali, Chinese New Year.

Books for older children and for adult information

Cass-Beggs, B. (1983) *A Musical Calendar of Festivals*, London: Ward Lock Educational.
Folk songs for feast days and holidays from around the world.
Didgeway, J. (1986) *Festive Occasions*, Oxford: Oxford University Press
World-wide festivals, teamed with relevant recipes.
Jaffrey, M. (1985) *Seasons of Splendour*, London: Pavilion Books.
Tales, myths, legends of India, including much on celebrations.
SHAP *Calendar of Religious Festivals*. Published annually by the Shap
Working Party, 7 Alderbrook Road, Solihull, West Midlands, B91 19H.
Festival series, Hove, E. Sussex: Wayland.
Includes books on Carnival, Harvest and Thanksgiving, Hallowe'en, New Year; Christian, Jewish, Muslim, Hindu, Sikh, and Buddist festivals.
Religious Topic series, Hove, E. Sussex: Wayland.
Includes books on Birth Customs, Marriage Customs, Feasting and Fasting, Initiation Rites.

Work Packs

(Age range is indicated by I: infant, J: junior, but they all contain material which can be adapted.)
Chinese New Year, Multi-Cultural Education Centre, Bishop Road, Bristol BS7 8LS.
Contains information and sheets for photocopying on: the twelve-year calendar, games, food, chopsticks, art; stories, some examples of script and numbers. (I)
Chinese New Year, (1986), London/Basingstoke: Commonwealth Institute/Macmillan Education.
Fact book, teacher's notes, wallsheets. (J)
Diwali, Minority Groups Support Service, Southfields Old School, South Street, Hillfields, Coventry CU1 5EJ.
Slides and commentary on Rama and Sita; worksheets for photocopying; 'Happy Diwali' in English, Gujerati, Hindi and Punjabi. Traditional geometric and symbolic floor patterns: Rangoli and Alpana. (I)
Diwali, Multi-Cultural Education Centre, Bishops Road, Bristol BS7 8LS.
Teacher's information, worksheets. Areas covered include: clothes, musical instruments, some script, art and activities. (I/J)

Eid, Multi-Cultural Education Centre, Bishops Road, Bristol BS7 8LS.
   Information and sheets for photocopying on: prayer, food, dress,
   jewellery, mehndi patterns, Islamic geometric patterns, Urdu
   script and numbers.   (I/J)
Festival of Holi, (1980), Minority Groups Support Service, Southfields
   Old School, South Street, Hillfields, Coventry CU1 5EJ.
   Story of Holi (the Hindu Spring Festival).   (I)
   The International Picture Library produces posters and slides on
   some festivals.

   There are many more books and packs available; most
Teachers' Centres, Multi-Cultural Education Centres, and
School Library Services will carry a good variety of resources
on at least the better-known festivals.

Illustrations of Celebrations topics

Plate 4.1 Birth is a universal occasion for celebration. Studying birth
rites associated with many cultures, here and in other countries,
shows that they have many points in common.

Plate 4.2 One part of a topic on bonfires looked at the role which they play in ceremonies in many cultures, here and elsewhere.

Figure 3 Sample topic web, 'Communications'

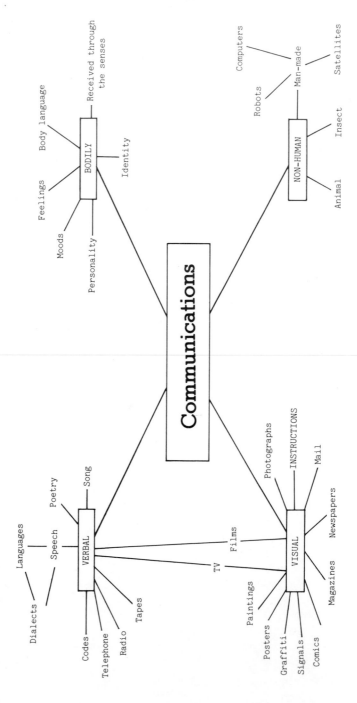

Figure 4 Supplementary topic web on Communications, 'Instructions'

Theme 2: Communications

Since Communications covers such a huge area, a web for just one possible topic, Instructions, has been included to illustrate what might be a manageable area for a single topic. Teachers will be able to use the wide scope of Communications topics to fit the exact needs of their classes.

Communications could prove an interesting medium through which to explore bias, innuendo, unconscious manipulation, reinforcement of stereotypes and prejudices, the impartiality or otherwise of the media, and so on. The fact that many of these features are used on both sides of arguments can be well illustrated through some Communication topics. These could be the vehicle for a closer look at language and languages, or at the subtleties that body language and expression bring to the spoken word. Communication through travel has not been touched upon here but some aspects of this are considered in Theme 3: Journeys.

Ethnic diversity may be included quite naturally in most areas of communications topics: by looking at a variety of languages, perhaps those which are spoken locally or in Britain; by including newspapers, magazines, comics, posters, and books in several languages; by looking at communication through art forms across cultures; by using stamps, maybe from children's own collections; by looking at television communications, using programmes made by and featuring people of many cultures. Efforts should also be made to ensure that friezes, class books, source material, and so on include people from minority British cultures in authentic detail of features, hair, clothing, colour, etc.

Teacher aims

* To bring out the wide similarities in universal communication,
* to look at the variations,
* to extend the topic to include most subject areas.

Pupil objectives

* To enable the children to understand and appreciate:

WHY people communicate
— to make and maintain relationships,
— to gain and pass on information,
— to express feelings,
— to prevent conflict.

WHEN people communicate
— all of the time, asleep and awake, consciously and unconsciously.

WHAT people communicate
— feelings,
— moods,
— information, facts,
— opinions,
— scandal, rumour, gossip,
— untruths.

WHERE people communicate
— everywhere.

HOW people communicate
— body language, expressions,
— speech,
— songs, music, poetry,
— tapes, discs,
— television, video,
— radio,
— newspapers, magazines, comics,
— telephone, satellite, cable,
— letters, telex, fax,
— signals, flags, Morse,
— Braille.

Non-human communication
— animal noises, gestures, bird-song, bees and ants,
— robots, computers.

Communications: a breakdown through curriculum subject areas

Reading and writing

These play a very central part in many Communication topics. Here, as in all topic work, children can be encouraged to use books as source material and to learn to find and extract relevant information from them.

Various examples of scripts could be looked at – both ways of writing English and scripts of other languages – and the children could try writing and reading them.

Poetry, rhymes, and story

These are mediums of communication which can be used in their own right, or looked at more analytically, to help the children to gain an insight into how they work as communications, and what can be communicated through them.

Topics on other areas of communication can be illustrated by using appropriate stories, rhymes, and poems, and the children can be encouraged to use these forms for their own creative writing.

Language

The mechanics of language could be examined at various levels, as could the ways that dialects, accents, social class, and so on affect what language communicates. The commonalities between languages – how similar certain words are, for example – is an interesting area, as is the huge range of human languages. Various scripts may be used, and alphabets compared, and children could invent their own languages and ways of writing them.

Other forms of 'language', such as body language (moods, feelings, expressions, body position and spacing), animal 'languages', and mechanical 'languages' (codes, signals, signs), could all be, or form part of, Communication topics.

Maths

The 'language' of number and the scripts in which number is communicated could be looked at. Children could invent their own number scripts. Mathematical codes could be fun to play with and might lead to investigating alternatives to 'base ten' work. This in turn leads to the translation of language into numbers for satellite and computer communications.

Maths can be part of other sorts of communications topics. For example, costings, and comparison of costings, can be done for postage, telephones, newspapers, etc. Sets, graphs, and charts can be used at many points in these topics. Weighing and measuring might be applicable for the correct postage rates, or for the weights of various newspapers.

Science

Human science is involved in the part that our senses play in communications, and social science in thinking about our common human need to communicate. The mechanics of animal and insect communication (both sending and receiving) could be looked at. The technology involved in methods of communication, such as printing, television, and satellites, could be investigated to a depth to suit the children's needs and stages of development.

Geography

Geography plays a part in many Communication topics. The suitability or unsuitability of some forms of communication for various parts of the world could help the children to recognize some less obvious reasons for differing rates of economic development between countries. Geographic reasons for poverty and wealth, and the effect of climate are relevant here, too.

How geography and climate affect, and have affected, the materials used for communications (for example, the use of linen, wood, rice, stone, and slate for 'paper') could be investigated.

The international reach of satellites and the ability of rocket technology to extend 'geography' into space could be included in some communication topics.

History

The history of communications and the discovery of new ways to communicate across cultures would find a place in some topics. Looking into the historic facts of poverty, wealth, war, conquest, colonization, as they affect communications, might help children to think with a wider perspective about some causative factors of our present world situation. Looking at how historical facts are communicated – going back before the written word – would stretch children well beyond their own and their family's lifespans.

R.E.

Religious communications could well form a complete topic, perhaps taking those methods which are common across many faiths, such as fasting, feasting, prayer, meditation, chanting, singing, and music.

Equally, religious forms of these areas could form part of a wider topic. It might be possible to consider what is communicated and how, and also unorthodox ways of doing so.

Artwork

Communications through art forms and across cultures, and our changing and developing abilities to perceive, would be interesting here. Children could try out different methods and perhaps invent their own.

Many language scripts are considered art forms in their own right. Calligraphy from various countries could be included and experimented with.

Most aspects of a communications topic could be illustrated on a class, group or individual level.

Music

Communication through music is a huge area by itself. Looking at what different music styles express, again across cultures, would be interesting and children could choose one through which to express themselves.

Ways of communicating music could be looked at: written music, taped and recorded music, live music, and so on.

Dance, movement, and drama

Children may investigate what they are able to communicate

through these forms. They could also use them to illustrate parts of communication topics, for example making up mimes to represent a printing press either individually or in groups, or dramatizing stores from the topic.

Communications: some resources

Resources from the children

Children can collect and bring in lots of things: stamps, postcards, other cards, magazines, comics, newspapers, and instructions in languages other than English; pictures that communicate feelings; tapes and records; articles that communicate feelings to them.

Resources in the local and wider community

Examples of varying accents, dialects, and language could be recorded from within the school and from the wider community. There might be parents or local people who work in one of the areas covered by the topic and who are willing to come and talk about it and demonstrate it.

There may be a television or radio studio or a newspaper office or printing press close enough to visit.

A mime artist or dance company might be invited to visit.

Published resources

Languages and scripts

Many of the books listed under 'Language diversity' will be useful here.

Bodily communication

Some of the material in the sections on 'Personal and Social Development' relate to bodily communications: for example, the ACER Project packs, *Words and Faces* and *Ourselves*, and the A. & C. Black/ILEA *People Around Us* Project Pack, Unit 1.

Other areas of this theme can be resources by using factual books on particular areas, such as television, the past, a film.

Illustrations of communications topics

Plate 4.3
Discovering how
the Euro-tunnel
would improve
European
communications
included looking
into the mechanics
of building it, and
the companies on
both sides of the
channel which
would be involved
in the work.

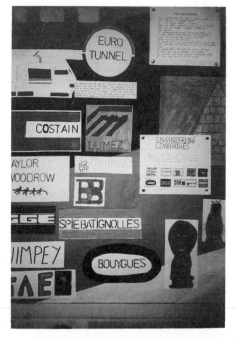

Plate 4.4 Children here were interested in how, and what, paintings communicate. This display explored how one artist communicated human emotions.

Figure 5 Sample topic web, 'Journeys'

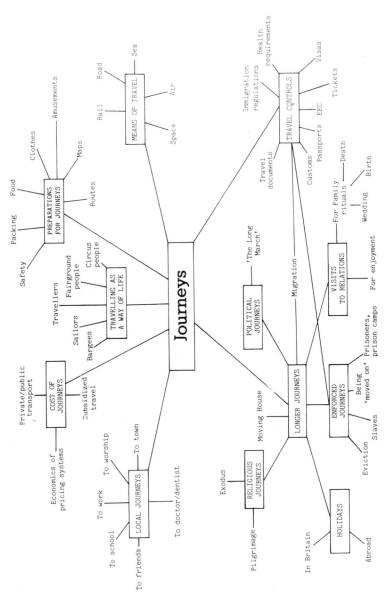

Theme 3: Journeys

The topic area of Journeys can lead children from familiar starting points towards a deeper understanding of the basic similarities of human life: everybody makes journeys, although the
details of them may vary. The focus of a particular topic could
be either broad enough to cover, say, all religious journeys, or
concentrated on a much smaller part, such as the food used for
journeys.

Ethnic diversity may be introduced very easily into the fabric
of a Journeys topic. The cultural diversity of Britain can be
unobtrusively included by choosing and making illustrations
that contain authentic details of black and Asian Britons as
well as other minority cultures and white Britons. Thus, for
example, a collage of an airport, which represents the ethnic
mix of British people, can be made, taking care that minority-
culture Britons are not predominantly shown in secondary
roles, such as cleaners or baggage-handlers. A topic on local
journeys could well feature a British Asian family making the
journeys, or those going to a dentist, doctor, or school could
be met there by black or Asian dentists, doctors, or headteachers (*not* by black or Asian assistants or cleaners). A
Journeys topic might be a good place to include sympathetic
work on Traveller families and other people who travel as a
way of life, concentrating on points of similarity rather than on
differences. Again, a Local Journeys topic could look at local
journeys in Britain and find all the similarities and variations
between them and local journeys in other countries. Care
should be taken to draw positive impressions from what might
superficially be seen as worse standards in some other countries. For example, where some journeys are undertaken by
animal power, the suitability of this for the prevailing conditions should be studied, the positive environmental aspects
pointed out, the advantages of a slower pace of life
appreciated, and so on. Conversely, the negative side of
mechanized transport could well be considered.

A topic that is wider ranging contains many obvious places to
ensure that the ethnic diversity of the world is included in the
children's work. Once again, the impression that the chosen
material makes on the children should be carefully weighed,
balancing any negative images and repairing omissions.

Teacher aims

* To bring out the world-wide element in the human experience of journeying,
* to look at the various ways in which similar ends are achieved,
* to incorporate work from most subject areas into the topic.

Pupil objectives

* To enable the children to understand and appreciate:

WHY people make journeys
— for and to work,
— for school,
— for pleasure: sight-seeing, visits, holidays,
— because they are compelled to: soldiers in wars, slaves, refugees, prisoners,
— for economic reasons: 'guest-workers', 'brain drain',
— for religious reasons: pilgrimages, etc.,
— as a way of life: Traveller families, bargees, fair and circus people.

WHEN they travel
— daily, in normal course of life,
— at holiday times,
— at times of national and international disruptions,
— for national and international 'happenings': music festivals, Olympics, conferences.

WHAT they travel in
— road transport,
— rail transport,
— air transport,
— sea transport,
— space transport,
— a mixture of two or more carriers.

WHERE people travel
— within their local environment,
— within their own country,
— to other parts of the world,
— to space.

HOW they travel
— alone,
— with family and friends,
— with luggage?
— with food?

Journeys: a breakdown through curriculum subject areas

Reading and writing

Reading and writing are vital to this topic, as to all others. In certain ways, the topic lends itself to experimenting with different ways of setting down information and with various styles of writing. Information gathered from parts of the topic could be written up in chart form (as tables or lists), 'cartoon' captions, pictures to be 'read', in report style, in forms of spoken language, in creative writing forms, in verse. Reading for information and pleasure could cover similar areas.

Poetry, rhymes, and story

Much published material is available on many aspects of Journey topics. Some, about historic journeys and journeys of 'discovery', could be used to help the children to look critically at what they are being told: for whom were the journeys of 'discovery' made? what were the results of discovery for the discovered?

   These subject areas offer good opportunities to delve deeper into the emotions involved in journeys: anticipation, expectancy, fear, joy, sorrow, and so on.

Language

Language diversity is a natural element of some Journey topics which range world wide. Children can be encouraged to project themselves into the feelings of people who come to Britain and cannot understand us, also of ourselves when we travel to areas where we cannot be understood. Various scripts could be included. Local variations in speech might be included, especially if the children have varying accents or use varying dialects.

There is a whole range of language related to travel and journeys which the children can be encouraged to discover and use.

Maths

Money, speed, distance, time and time zones, all have a part in Journey topics. Units of measurement from more than one country would fit well here. There is a lot of scope for using graphs, sets, and charts to record information from these topics: types of vehicles seen in ten minutes, how we come to school, where does your family originate from?

Science

The mechanics of travel could be investigated, and the children could invent 'vehicles' and sources of power, using, for instance, gradients and rubber bands.

The fuels which are used, and the environmental effects of using them, could be looked at. Animal power could be shown to have advantages here.

Navigational aids, the principles of food preservation for long journeys, and the effects of air and sea currents are just some of the areas which might be included in these topics.

Geography

Maps, plotting, and route-finding, at many levels of ability, fall naturally into the scope of Journeys topics. Trade routes, trade winds, and the cash crops which caused the journeys to come into being could be looked at; similarly, famine, drought, and unemployment could be studied as reasons for some journeys.

History

The history of inventions which are connected with transport might be included; famous journeys and journeys of discovery could lead to looking at the inventions from more than one point of view. Colonization, the movement of slaves, immigration, and migration could be treated in the same way. Studies could be made of the way in which our accepted concepts of the world have changed according to received opinion on the shape of the earth: for example, the 'flat earth' concepts, and how Great Britain and Europe are shown disproportionately large on many old maps. Future history could be anticipated by speculation on space travel, aided perhaps by insights into how attitudes to terrestrial travel have shaped world history.

R.E.

Religious journeys could fit into a variety of Journey topics: pilgrimages, processions, funerals, and so on. The religious significance of journeys in several British faiths would be an interesting area, and one which could be dealt with at varying levels to suit particular children. The reasons why religious leaders travel and the effects of their journeys would bring world faiths into present lives.

Artwork

Children could make local maps, and design imaginary ones; they could look at old maps and maps from other countries. Areas such as perspective, distance, and light could be investigated through art and craft. The decorative arts of Travellers, bargees, etc. could be looked at. Many art skills can be combined to produce class, group, and individual work to illustrate Journey topics.

Music

Children can experience how movement is translated into music and can experiment with their own 'travelling' sounds. Songs about journeys and travelling can be learned, and parts of known songs, such as 'Yankee Doodle', can be studied from this angle.

Dance, movement, and drama

Children can experiment with how to portray movement and travelling in confined spaces; they can dramatize favourite stories; they can use these modes to recognize and express the emotions of journeys and travelling.

Journeys: some resources

Resources from the children

Children will be able to bring tickets for various journeys which they have taken: bus, rail, ferry, air; cards from people on holiday; photographs from holiday journeys. Perhaps they can contribute their own experiences of journeys, especially those children who have settled locally after coming from other areas or other countries.

Resources in the local and wider community

Parents and staff may have interesting experiences of journeys to recount; they may work in some branch of travel; their religion may give them knowledge of religious journeys.

Information about health, passport and visa requirements can be obtained from main post offices and the central passport offices.

The embassies and tourist offices of individual countries can supply details of their areas: road and rail maps, air routes, other means of travelling, and so on.

Travel agencies, bus, rail, and airline organizations can give pricing and timing details, and maps.

Published resources

There are many books available on particular aspects of travel. Most schools will have some. Unfortunately, most will not reflect the ethnic diversity within Britain but this omission can be corrected by a teacher who is aware of such a lack.

Books which encompass larger themes often include relevant material, e.g. many books on religion have sections on religious journeys. Journeys of 'discovery' will be found in history or adventure books; these will very often be biased and stereotyped and so should either be adapted by the teacher or not be used at all. Some might be used as teaching points but they should not be available for the children's free choice if they are very ethnocentric.

Children's books

There are many modern children's books about journeys which reflect the ethnic diversity of Britain. The following are three examples:

Bradman, T. and Brown, E. (1986) *Through My Window*, London: Methuen Children's Books.
For Infants.
Ganly, H. (1986) *Jyoti's Journey*, London: Andre Deutsch.
A picture book for Infants.
Paton Walsh, J. (1981) *Babylon*, London: Beaver (Arrow Books).
A picture book, for Infants.

The following books are just a sample of the many available which feature some aspect of journeys:

Bond, R. (1985) *Getting Granny's Glasses*, London: Blackbird (Julia MacRae Books).
A Hindi story, set in the Indian sub-continent, for older Infants.
Daley, N. (1985) *Not So Fast, Songololo*, London: Victor Gollancz.
A black South African story for Infants.
Marshal, J.V. (1979) *Walkabout*, London: Puffin.
An Australian outback adventure. Would make a good story to read to Junior children.
Naidoo, B. (1985) *Journey to Jo'burg*, London: Longman
About a journey by a 13-year old and his brother in South Africa who set out to find their mother. For reading to older Infants.
Searle, C. (compiler) (1983) *Wheel Around the World*, London: Macdonald.
A poetry book with at least one poem about a journey, in a sampan.

Illustrations of Journeys topics

Plate 4.5 Journeys by boat, by foot, and those undertaken by pigeons found a place in this frieze of the Tyne Suspension Bridge, which formed part of a 'Journeys' topic.

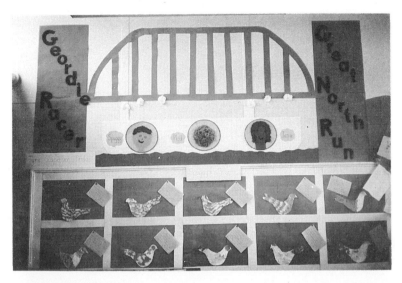

Plate 4.6 Journeys taken while emigrating were looked at in part of this topic which traced the children's family trees.

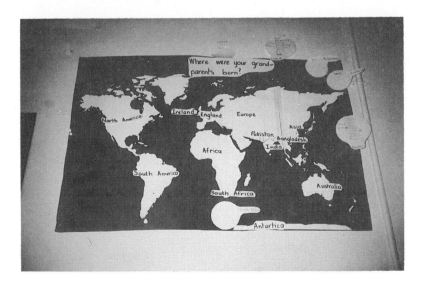

Figure 6 Sample topic web, 'Shelter and Homes'

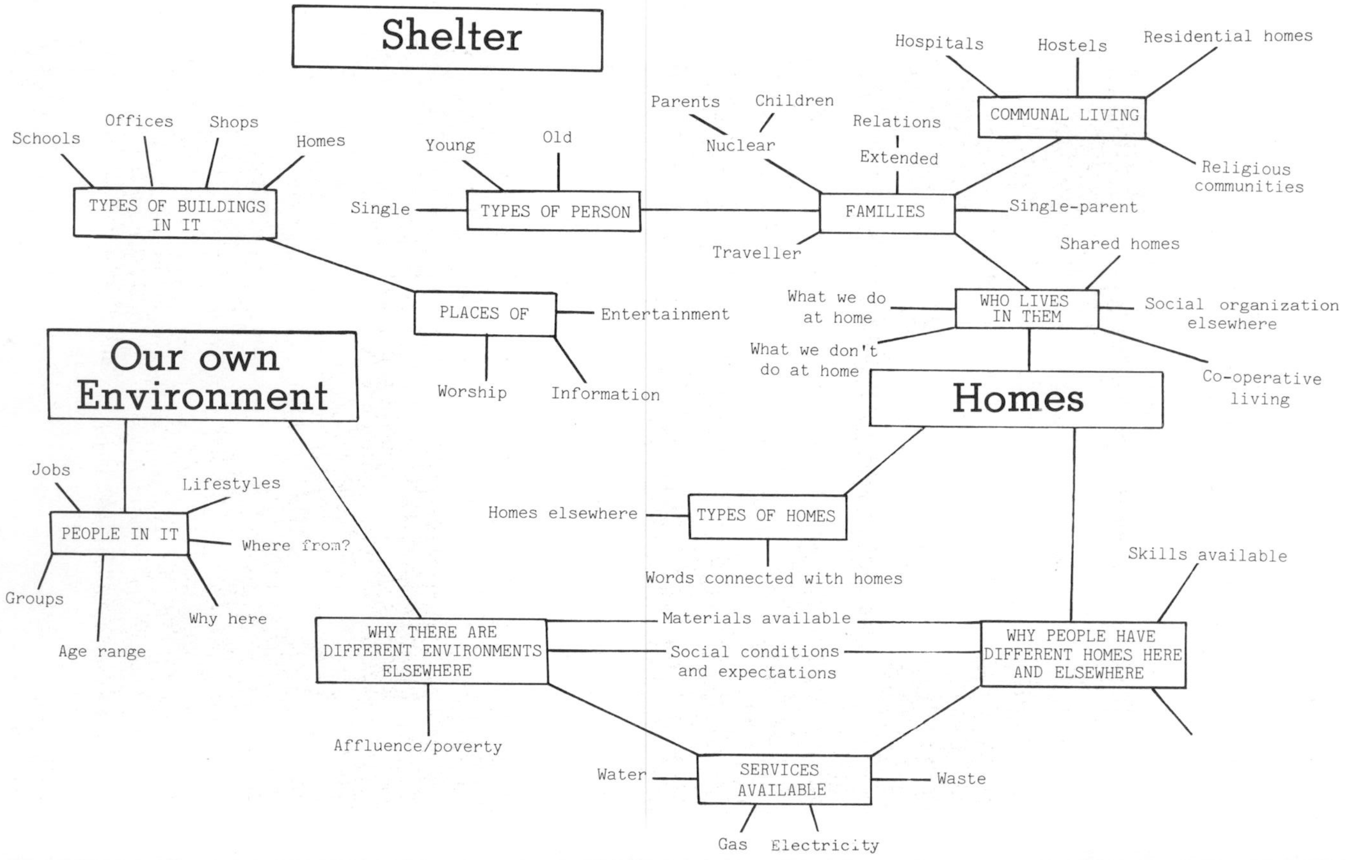

Theme 4: Shelter

Shelter can be the starting point for a wide variety of self-contained topics or it can form a part of other topics, such as Our Place, Ourselves, Homes.

The diversity of British cultures can be reflected in the materials that are used and produced through Shelter topics, by using source materials which reflect many of our cultures and by portraying people of these cultures authentically in illustrations for the chosen topic. Within topics such as Families, British Muslim families or British West Indian families could be studied rather than looking at Muslim or West Indian families living in other countries.

As the topic web shows, Shelter topics could lead children to look at their society from more than one point of view, and to begin to delve into the 'cause and effect' aspects of wealth, poverty, social conditions, and expectations. Children need gradual introductions to these areas, which might be completely new angles of thought for them. Topics such as these, which are grounded in the children's own experiences and extend outwards from there, help to make variations from their own norms accessible and permissible.

As Shelter is such a very wide area, one part of it, Homes, has been selected to be Theme 5. A joint Resources list appears at the end of Theme 5 on p. 93.

Teacher aims

* To bring out the universality of the human need for shelter,
* To look at the variety that there is in achieving shelter,
* To cover most subject areas through the topic.

Pupil objectives

* To enable the children to understand and appreciate:

WHY we need shelter
— for protection from climate,
— for protection from animals and insects,
— for privacy; for psychological reasons,
— for organizational reasons: collecting workers together to work.

WHEN we need shelter
— shelter of caring parents for babies and children,
— shelter of children and relatives for ageing parents,
— shelter of friends for everyone,
— shelter of the caring State in times of crisis,
— shelter of compassionate world in times of international crisis,
— for work, play, living, dying.

WHAT shelter is
— homes: the huge variety in Britain and the rest of the world; variety in types, construction, materials used, services available,
— the Welfare State and other forms of this in other countries,
— charity,
— religion: sanctuary, shelter of belief,
— economic shelter: work and money,
— alternative ways of living: communes, collectives, Traveller people.

WHERE we need shelter
— most humans need the shelter of a place to return to,
— in virtually all aspects of human life.

HOW we
— secure shelter for ourselves,
— offer shelter: hospitality, friendship,
— try to ensure shelter for all: homelessness, bed-and-breakfast families, unemployment,
— pass on shelter: inheritance laws and traditions.

Shelter: a breakdown through curriculum subject areas

Reading and writing

These are both vital to this as to all topics. Points made under this heading in other themes apply equally here.

Reading related to topic work is a good way of introducing children to critical reading: reading with an increasingly aware mind which is not content to accept material passively, just as it is presented. Getting children to draw from their own experience in order to test what they are being told is a skill that can be developed from an early age; it is an essential skill for making balanced use of information which is received through the various media.

Reading, rhymes, and story

Many of these items will contain parts, however incidental, which are relevant to Shelter topics. Focusing on the particular shelter element that is being studied can bring new light to bear on familiar material.

Families and aspects of British urban life are often featured in the many good multi-cultural story, picture, and poetry books which are now available.

Language

The numerous words and phrases that describe shelter, and the breadth that that one word can cover can be interesting areas to examine. These activities could be the basis for children's creative writing.

Words in other languages and scripts might be found to illustrate various Shelter topics.

Maths

Many aspects of Shelter topics give occasion to use and manipulate numbers: looking at the sizes of communities, at population numbers and rates of increase, at family sizes, house sizes, and so on. Money and economics can be brought in by looking at the costs of shelter in its widest sense, and by looking at the costs of withholding shelter: looking at the costs of unemployment, for example, which include the loss to tax revenues, the reduction of purchasing power, and the cost of unemployment pay. The accumulative, and hidden, costs of poor housing to the NHS, to employers, and so on would be an interesting area to look at.

Science

Science elements could include developments that have influenced communities in areas such as health, medicine, communications, utility services, the media, and so on.

Looking at why modern scientific benefits are not available to all people, in Britain and the rest of the world, and why not all developments are desirable in an ecology – and conservation – conscious world would broaden children's outlooks.

Social science elements could find a place in Shelter topics: delving into how communities do and do not work (perhaps taking the class or school as an example of community); thinking about groups, crowds, and individuals and how people's behaviour changes in various settings.

Geography

Geographical positions influences shelter in many ways, from the type of physical shelter possible, through the type of state-provided shelter, such as welfare and health services. The geographical roots of poverty and wealth and how these affect shelter could be included. The effects of climate and of man-made and natural disasters on shelter in its many senses, and how we cope with them, could be studied, perhaps through current events when the topic is being worked on.

History

The historical development of many aspects of shelter and the effect on them of events in history could be investigated: for example, the effects of the Black Death on population numbers world wide; the effects of invasion and conquest on whole peoples; how slavery affected the countries that provided and received slaves, in human terms and in terms of poverty and wealth; how modern wars influence shelter, how future wars may do so.

R.E.

Religion continues to play an important part in many areas of shelter. Whole societies are modelled on religious teachings: their lifestyles, clothing, food, education, recreation, family size, and so on.

The similarities and variations between the many religious communities in Britain, and how they are adapting and changing, could be studied through Shelter topics.

Artwork

Children could experiment with various methods of illustrating Shelter topics, such as large-scale models, pictorial flow charts, montages, and so on. They could be asked to illustrate their own concepts of shelter before one particular area is chosen for the topic.

Some Shelter topics could include an investigation of the designs of homes and other buildings, in Britain and other parts of the world.

Music

Many familiar songs and much modern 'cult' music will contain incidental references to shelter. Children can be helped to recognize these. They will enjoy creating their own music, in their favourite style, about parts of the topic in which they are particularly interested, and expressing through music the emotions that are engendered by parts of the topic.

The basic human desire to make music can be drawn out in some Shelter topics.

Dance, movement, and drama

Children can be very inventive here, both creating dramas, mimes, and so on to contrast communities – ancient, modern, futuristic – and choosing other areas of the topic in which to do this work.

Dance, movement, and drama as a common factor of many societies and communities and their unifying effect on people, can be examined.

Illustrations of Shelter topics

Plate 4.7 Shelter was just one of the areas covered in a large topic on 'Survival' which looked at what all people need to survive.

Plate 4.8 Looking at the services which most of us take for granted as part of the domestic shelter which we enjoy can lead naturally to considering whether they are available to all people.

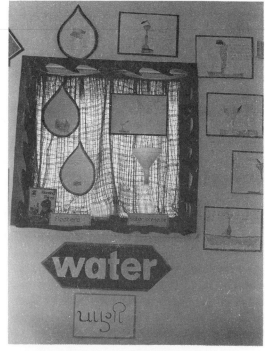

Figure 7 Alternative sample topic web, 'Homes'

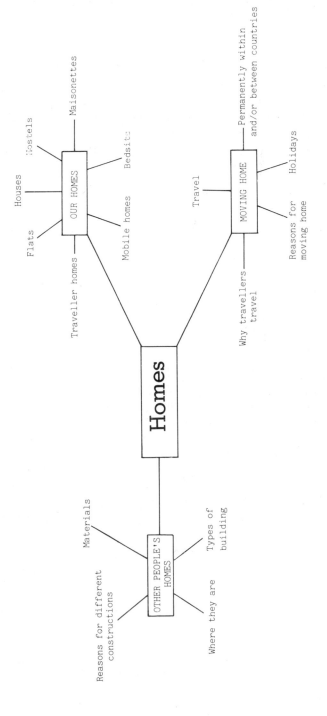

Theme 5: Homes

Homes topics, and others like them, are often used in schools and can be good vehicles for utilizing the children's own experiences in order to emphasize the fundamental commonalities of homes for all humans. Starting from basic needs, it is easy to accept that there is a variety of ways to fulfil them, according to local conditions. Thus, the variety of homes world wide is understandable and reasonable when such things as the local availability of materials and the climate are considered. The various concepts of who constitutes 'family' can be seen to influence house size, and diverse tastes can be seen to play a part in the common desire to make homes attractive and comfortable. Comparative wealth and poverty can be shown to affect people's homes the world over.

It is very important here, as in all topics, to give a balanced picture of all countries, so that children do not reinforce stereotypes which they may have that all people from less developed countries live in shacks, or that all 'white' or European people live in modern homes. In topics which start from children's own experience, it is essential to include all of the types of homes in which the children live and also to include types of homes of which the children may not have personal experience, such as caravans, communal houses, and bed and breakfast accommodation. Teachers have the delicate tasks here of ensuring that all homes are valued and of helping the children to realize that the essential nature of a home is not determined by material possessions.

Ethnic diversity can be introduced into Homes topics by using source materials which feature people of many cultures, both British and world wide. Points such as who first discovered glass-making, the Romans having had efficient central heating, Scandinavians having very good methods of insulation and power saving, certain woods coming from which country, when they are introduced or discovered at relevant times in the topics, include world-wide influences without over-emphasizing them.

The diverse nature of British society is included quite naturally by ensuring that a broad mix of people appears in all of the ordinary parts of the topics and not as special points. Thus, a British family of Chinese extraction could be chosen to illustrate a family living in a house, a black British family could be shown going on holiday, and so on. Details of skin tones, facial features, hairstyles, and clothing must be accurate.

Teacher aims

* To look at homes in a wide context,
* To look at the common features of homes and at the variety within that commonality,
* To cover most subject areas through the topic.

Pupil objectives

* To enable the children to understand and appreciate:

WHY we need homes
— for protection against climate,
— as a collective base for a family; as a base for individuals,
— to cater for psychological needs for privacy, ownership, safety, stability,
— to cater for physical requirements of sleep, food, hygiene,
— as a social base.

WHEN we need homes
— throughout our whole lives: babyhood, childhood, adult life, old age,
— wherever we settle,
— temporarily, during periods of personal, national, or world-wide unrest or instability,
— when we travel.

WHAT a home is
— somewhere to sleep and to keep ourselves clean,
— a place in which to raise a family,
— somewhere to 'grow roots', become established,
— a place of stability, acceptance,
— different things to different people,
— to some people, it does not exist or is the opposite of most people's expectations,
— a flat, bed-sit, house, maisonette, mobile home, boat, hut, shack, bed and breakfast accommodation, etc.

WHERE we need homes
— wherever there are people in the world,
— near to employment,
— near to relations, schools, shops, entertainment,
— en-route, when travelling,
— in holiday destinations,
— some people need homes 'away from everything'; some need homes and do not have them.

HOW we
— find a home,
— finance it,
— look after it,
— lose it,
— share it,
— move home.

Homes: a breakdown through curriculum subject areas

Reading and writing

Homes topics, as with other topic areas, can provide a purposeful focus for reading and writing and, if carefully planned and handled, can ensure valuable practice for reading and writing skills in an interesting and unthreatening way. In reading, children can practise the skills of extracting meaning from illustrations, of using context clues to read unknown words, of anticipating what comes next, and so on. In writing, the children's personal knowledge of their homes can provide them with well-known subjects to write about, and with starting points for creative writing.

Poetry, rhymes, and story

Homes feature, often indirectly, in many poems, rhymes, and stories for young children. Because all of the children have a considerable experience of homes (and are therefore starting from a known base of information), stories, rhymes, and poems around Homes topics are good for them to practise their skills of listening, recall, and re-telling. Homes is also a good area (because it is easily understood in some form by the children) in which to draw out basic human commonalities;

poems, rhymes, and stories are interesting ways of presenting these commonalities.

Language

The words for 'home' in various languages and scripts can be shown, and the many words which we use for homes can be discovered. Words to describe homes can be listed and used by children in their writing. The homes (origins) of languages might also be looked at.

Maths

Plans of homes might be drawn, using measuring and area. Pattern and shape can be discovered in many parts of homes. Graphs, sets, and charts can be drawn in many Homes topics: how many people live in flats, in houses, . . .? how many children have dogs, cats, . . .?, and so on.

The economics of homes might be touched upon; similarly, the economics of not having a home. For example, how much does it cost to make a cup of tea at home and how much does it cost if you have to buy each cup outside because you either do not have a home or cannot cook there?

Science

The materials that are used for making homes, in Britain and other countries, can be looked at, and the positive advantages of some materials which are unusual to us, may be highlighted. How some materials protect against heat, cold, moisture; how some structures resist earthquakes or winds; how the utility services work; how people manage without utility services: each of these areas and more could be covered. Homes of the future, using solar energy, robots, and 'armchair' shopping and banking could be speculated upon.

Geography

The effect of climate, geography, and local materials on homes could be looked at. Moving home often involves some geographic changes, as do the life-styles of travelling people:

bargees, circus and fair people, Travellers, and so on.

History

The historical development of, and changes in, homes could be studied, as could inventions which have altered our concepts of home. The historic reasons for poverty and wealth which effect homes today on a local, national, and world-wide scale would be interesting to look at. The children could draw on their parents' and grandparents' knowledge to see how the contents of homes have changed.

R.E.

The homes of religions – Jerusalem. Mecca, Rome, etc. – and religious homes, such as temples, chapels, shrines, and synagogues, would introduce other interpretations for the word 'home'. Religious influences on homes could be looked at, as could religious reasons for moving home.

Highlighting the central parts that homes and families play in many religions would show another area of fundamental similarity between people.

Artwork

The children could practise many art skills in a Homes topic: designing material for furnishings, using batik for example, or doing 'rubs' and prints of articles and surfaces at home. Patterns and decorations which are favoured by particular cultures could be looked at; likewise, the design of furniture and machinery could be considered. Children will enjoy modelling homes in various materials and making pictures and collages of them.

Music

The homes (origins) of various music styles can be investigated, and the reasons why so many are practised in Britain. Homes feature in many songs, as do feelings about homes and moving home. Children may create music to illustrate many parts of Home topics.

Dance, movement, and drama

The homes (origins) of dance styles could be looked at and some of the styles could be tried out.

Dance, movement, and drama are good media for expressing the emotions involved with homes: moving, returning, losing them, and so on.

Shelter and homes: some resources

Resources from the children

Children can contribute their own experiences in all of the areas that are used in the topics; with help they will be able to draw out the basic similarities and the variety within them. They can collect pictures from magazines, travel booklets, and postcards; they may have toys, models, and construction toys at home (model villages, Lego, brick kits) which they can lend.

Resources in the local and wider community

The local environment itself is useful as a starting point for many possible topics in these areas; interesting contrasts may be made between the immediate environment and adjacent localities.

Staff, parents, and local people may well have relevant knowledge and/or materials which they would share with the children: for example, people who have moved house for various reasons, or who have lived in very different houses and communities. People with different types and sizes of family might contribute facts and figures: 'nuclear' families, 'extended' families, 'communal' families, traveller families.

It might be possible to find a variety of jobs done by local people – builders, carpenters, shop-keepers – or perhaps relevant local work-places, such as a water-works or sewage plant.

Whichever area is taken for the topic, it should be fairly easy to draw resources for it from the locality.

In predominantly white areas, teachers must be ready to extend each area to include the ethnic diversity of Britain.

Published resources

Beans series, London: A. & C. Black.
    Some of the books in this series look at life in other countries;
    many of them show housing and other buildings.
Houses and Homes series (1987): titles *Building Homes, Homes in Cold
    Places, Homes in Hot Places, Homes on Water*, Hove, E. Sussex:
    Wayland.
    These well-illustrated books are aimed at 7–9 year olds but the
    material is adaptable for other ages.
My Village In . . . series, London: MacDonald.
    Looks at village life in Nepal, Morocco, and the Sahara (perhaps
    more titles to follow). For Juniors, but the material is adaptable.
Mayled, J. (1986) *Religious Buildings*, Religious Topic series, Hove, E.
    Sussex: Wayland.
    Again the material may be adapted to interest a wide age range.
Wood, S. (1982) *The World Around Us*, Macmillan Colour Library,
    Basingstoke: Macmillan Education.
    Looks at homes and the caring services, amongst other things.

All of the following children's books feature a particular
family and often show their homes.

Bennett, O. (1983) *Turkish Afternoon*, London: Hamish Hamilton.
    A British Turkish-Cypriot family.
Blakely, M. (1977) *Nahda's Family*, London: A. & C. Black.
    A British Muslim family, originally from Pakistan.
Crossfield Family (1978) *Seven of Us*, London: A. & C. Black.
    A British Jamaican family.
Knapp, C. (1979) *Shimon, Leah and Benjamin*, London: A. & C. Black.
    A British Jewish family.
Lyle, S. (1977) *Pavan is a Sikh*, London: A. & C. Black.
    A British Sikh family.
McCarty, N. (1977) *Rebecca is a Cypriot*, London: A. & C. Black.
    A British Greek-Cypriot family.
Mayled, J. (1986) *Family Life*, Religious Topic series, Hove, E. Sussex:
    Wayland.

The following seven books are by Joan Solomon and are
published by Hamish Hamilton:

        Bobbie's New Year: British Sikh family.
(1980) *Gifts and Almonds*: British Muslim family.
(1980) *Shabnum's Day Out*: British Muslim family.
(1981) *A Present for Mum*: British Asian family.
(1981) *Wedding Day*: British Hindu family.
(1984) *Sweet Tooth Sumil*: British Hindu family.
        News for Dad: British Sikh family.

Tsow, M. (1982) *A Day with Ling*, London: Hamish Hamilton.
   A British Chinese family.
Families Around the World series, Hove, E. Sussex: Wayland.
   Around twenty titles, aimed at 8–12 year olds, with plenty of
   photographs. Teachers could use the facts, simplified, for
   younger children.

Published materials in these areas need to be used very
sensitively, to ensure a balanced picture of the varied conditions in all countries. Resources that show stereotyped images
should either be fully discussed with the children or not be
used at all.

Illustrations of Homes topics

Plate 4.9 Ways of making bricks – a common element in many homes – looked at world-wide.

Plate 4.10 A Jewish story formed part of this Home topic, subtly widening children's horizons to acknowledge another common, human element of life

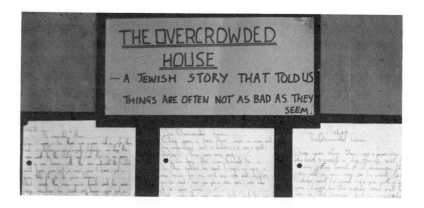

Figure 8 Sample topic web, 'Food'

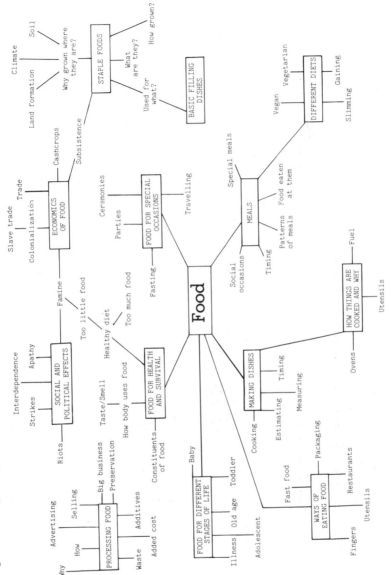

Figure 9 Supplementary topic web on Food, 'Basic filling dishes'

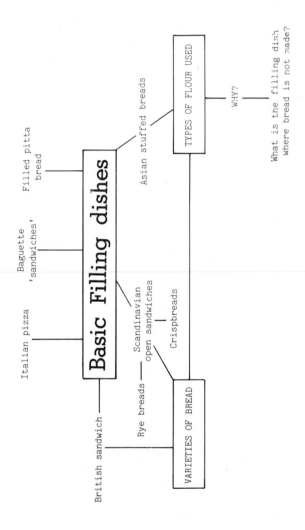

Theme 6: Food

This is a huge topic area which has links with others, such as Celebrations, Festivals, Journeys, Ourselves, Farming, and so on. The questions why, when, what, where, and how may be answered in many ways, reflecting teachers' and children's current interests, and not just as they are listed here.

One particular food or one family of food, such as vegetables, or one meal may be used as the complete topic. A sample Food topic on Basic Filling Dishes and an example of a resource list of published material mentioning bread has been included to illustrate the versatility of the whole area.

The ethnic diversity of Britain may be included in many ways in a Food topic: the variety of restaurants and take-aways that there are in Britain, the 'ethnic' foods that are now easily available almost everywhere, the cooking utensils from other cultures that are used here. Without the diverse nature of British society, we should not have this wealth of variety. As in all other themes, ethnic diversity can be included by ensuring that black and Asian Britons and people from other minority cultures are properly represented in resources, illustrations, and collages.

Almost all aspects of food lend themselves to a natural extension outwards from children's immediate experiences. Investigating the variety of food and cooking styles which is found in Britain leads on to discovering where they originate and how they arrived here. Looking at British basic food leads on to looking for food from other cultures which fulfils the same purposes. Using British basic cooking methods leads on to finding out which methods are common to other styles of cooking, and so on. Looking at the origins of food and at the variations within all of the basic similarities widens any Food topic to encompass the world and all of its cultures.

Current news items often involve food or the lack of it. Investigations into these items can help the children to develop critical abilities in relation to media presentation and can help them to get into the habit of delving below the surface of reported facts.

Looking at how some national eating and drinking habits influence life in other parts of the world illuminates the connections which exist between all peoples. For example, what effect does British demand for tea have on tea-producing countries, the standard of their living, the ecology of their countries? How might our demands be modified, and how would this help other people?

Teacher aims

* To show the common human need for food, and the variety of ways of satisfying that need,
* To show the wider social and political aspects of food,
* To incorporate work from most subject areas into the topic.

Pupil objectives

* To enable the children to understand and appreciate:

WHY we need food
— all people: to stay healthy and to be able to function; to keep warm.
— children: for growth as well.

WHEN we have food
— mealtimes: how these vary between cultures, classes and age-groups,
— at special occasions: celebrations, feasts, funerals, religious ceremonies,
— for some people: only when there has been a good enough harvest.

WHAT we eat
— types of food: proteins, etc.,
— various diets: vegetarian, slimming,
— special needs: religious, children, old people, sick people, allergies,
— too much, too little: why?

WHERE food is eaten and prepared
— at home: nuclear, extended, single parent, Traveller families,
— communally: restaurants, canteens, schools, colleges, soup-kitchens, feeding-centres, camps,
— factories: processed and prepared food, additives, flavourings.

WHERE food comes from
— land, sea,
— animals, insects, vegetables,
— various countries: cash crops, subsistence farming, food mountains, food economics,
— new technology: sources of textured protein; ways of using surpluses; fuel from sugars.

HOW we eat
— ways of eating various foods,
— ways of eating across cultures,
— economics of eating: how various patterns are maintained.

Food: a breakdown through curriculum subject areas

Reading and writing

These skills are integral to Food topics. As with other topics, Food topics are good areas within which to help children to discover the benefits of collaborative reading and writing: that more information can be utilized if several people cover various separate areas; that pooling ideas, co-operating, and discussing can lead to a more satisfying end-product; that, by working in groups, members can help each other at their own levels; and so on. Having an interesting end-product in mind, perhaps a communal book or poem, or a group drama or dance, gives an incentive to co-operating and sharing. Children need lots of practice in order for collaborative and group work to work well; topics provide unthreatening environments for such practice.

Poetry, rhymes, story

There is much written, directly and indirectly, about food and food-related activities, and so teachers should have no trouble in finding plenty of material that they can use. With a little thought, questioning and discussion can extend what might otherwise be mono-cultural references.

Many of the multi-cultural books now available refer to food, quite often in a British context.

Children will have a fund of relevant experience and a natural interest which will help their own creative writing on food topics.

Language

Many of the basic commonalities of food can be illustrated through language: by looking at foods common to many countries and discovering their names, by finding out the names of basically similar dishes, by seeing what meals are called in other countries, and so on.

The actual language and style of writing recipes could be looked at, as could the words used to describe the processes of food preparation. Words describing the sensations which we receive from all of our senses in relation to food would provide a rich collection for children's creative work.

Maths

As weighing and measuring fit easily into Food topics, graphs, charts, and sets can be drawn from many of them.

Time can be included in cooking, also in plant and animal life-cycles, and in the cycles of planting, growth, harvest, and decay.

Money can be included either by simply costing a dish or by looking at the more complex area of world economics. Many items which are usually hidden within statistics can be exposed, such as the costs of importing subsistence foods into countries where too much land is given over to cash crops.

Shape, pattern, and design can be included by looking at areas such as food packaging and food presentation.

Science

Experiments may be carried out on taste, smell, touch, and sound, and to discover the constituents of food. Factors which influence growth, and areas such as food additives, food preservation, and farm chemicals, may be examined.

Geography

What grows where (on land and sea) and why, and the influence that this has on national diets, can be studied. The sources of British food imports and the destinations of food exports can be plotted.

Looking at trade routes, cash crops, subsistence farming, starvation, famine, glut, and food mountains shows our global interconnections and the areas where more co-operation is required.

History

The history of human beings' move from being nomads to settled urban dwellers intimately involves many aspects of food. The uneven spread of these developments world wide could be considered. The connection of colonization with world food supplies, how food riots have affected world history, how the growth of the EEC and its food mountains are also doing so: these and many other areas could be covered.

R.E.

The importance of food in many religions, as it applies in Britain and other countries, may be studied. How do British people of various faiths follow their beliefs about food taboos, about when certain foods may be eaten, about fasting, about feasting? How do they obtain the foods that they need for religious observances? Do they have to compromise?

Religious involvement and help in areas of food shortages can also be looked at.

Artwork

The shape and pattern of and within foods from many countries can be studied and recorded. Children can experiment with packaging designs and can make food adverts. Food decoration across cultures can be studied and tried out. Some foods, food labels, and packages could be included in collages.

Music

Music and food seem natural companions. There are songs about food, rhymes and chants for ploughing, planting, winnowing, grinding, fishing activities, and so on. The children could invent their own, matching the chant to the rhythm of the actions.

Dance, movement, drama

Machine and human movements connected with food may be portrayed here. Traditional dances could be tried out, and areas of food topics dramatized.

Food: some resources

Resources from the children

The children can contribute a variety of experiences about all aspects of the topic: all will have tasted food from other cultures, many will have eaten food abroad, all will have experience of various meals and eating habits.

They can collect food packages from home, pictures of food, and samples of food, eating, and cooking utensils. They may be able to find books of recipes for food from various cultures. Most children will be able to bring things to grow: carrot tops, date stones, grape pips . . . things to taste, smell, touch.

Resources in the local and wider community

People in the community may be able to provide much information about various ways of cooking and eating; meal patterns; experiences of hunger and hardship; details of special diets, special foods, special occasions. Perhaps some people can provide other languages in which to name foods.

Local areas will probably have examples of food shops and restaurants, most of which will contain food that originated in other countries. It might be possible to find and visit local food factories, dairies, bakers, and processors, and to find people to talk about their jobs in the food industry.

Food is a topic where, even in an all-white area, ethnic diversity in resources should be easily achieved.

Published resources

There are many books on all aspects of food. With care, and by using modern publications, it should be possible to provide balanced, ethnically diverse materials to reflect Britain and the world realistically. Biased and stereotyped books should either be fully discussed with the children or not be used at all.

The following is a list of children's books which contain references to food, often in the context of families living in Britain.

Bennett, O. (1983) *Turkish Afternoon*, London: Hamish Hamilton
Turkish sweets, food, coffee-making.
Blakely, M. (1977) *Nahda's Family*, London: A. & C. Black.
Pakistani food.
Crossfield Family (1978) *Seven of Us*, London: A. & C. Black.
A Jamaican market, vegetables, food.
Knapp, C. (1979) *Shimon, Leah and Benjamin*, London: A. & C. Black.
Kosher food.
Lyle, S. (1977) *Pavan is a Sikh*, London: A. & C. Black.
References to Punjabi food.
McCarty, N. (1977) *Rebecca is a Cypriot*, London: A. & C. Black.
References to food, coffee.

The following three books are by Joan Solomon and are published by Hamish Hamilton:

Bobbie's New Year: Food for New Year, Sikh.
(1980) *Gifts and Almonds*: Rice
(1984) *Sweet Tooth Sumil*: Lots about food to celebrate Diwali.

Tsow, M. (1982) *A Day with Ling*, London: Hamish Hamilton.
Chinese cooking/supermarket.
(1984) *Phototalk* series, London: ILEA Learning Resources Branch.
Mealtime with Lily: Chinese Food.
Sarqua and Shan go Shopping: Indian food.

Bread: some resources

Bennett, O. (1983) *Turkish Afternoon*, London: Hamish Hamilton.
Turkish bread – corek (*chor-rek*).
Knapp, C. (1979) *Shimon, Leah and Benjamin*, London: A. & C. Black.
Reference to matzos – unleavened bread.
Lyle, S. (1977) *Pavan is a Sikh*, London: A. & C. Black.
Reference to Punjabi bread.
McCarty, N. (1977) *Rebecca is a Cypriot*, London: A. & C. Black.
Reference to Greek bread.

The following three books are by Joan Solomon and are published by Hamish Hamilton:

Bobbie's New Year: Sikh, making unleavened bread.
News for Dad: Making *chappatis*.
(1984) *Sweet Tooth Sumil*: Mentions *puries* – Indian bread.

(1984) *Phototalk* series, London: ILEA Learning Resources Branch.
    Eating with Bader and Nabil: Flat Turkish bread – corek.

Games

There are quite a number of simulations and active learning games which look into world food supply and distribution. Below are just two examples. Both Oxfam and Christian Aid have more.

The World Feast Game (1982), Christian Aid Education Department, P.O. Box 1, London, SW9 8BH.
    This is intended for children of 10–12 years over a wide range of abilities. It aims to illustrate the uneven distribution of food around the world.

The World in a Supermarket Bag (1987), Oxfam, 274 Banbury Road, Oxford, OX2 7DZ.
    This is for 7–11 year olds and aims to illustrate the world-wide sources of our food in Britain, to start thoughts about 'trade' and what goes into the cost of food, and to show how poorer countries feed us and our pets.

Illustrations of Food topics

Plate 4.11 The story of the 'Runaway Chappati' – in the style of the 'Gingerbread Man' – was used by this class to illustrate a topic on bread.

Plate 4.12 The children here found that we owe one of our staple foods to the people of another country.

Figure 10 Sample topic web, 'Hats and head coverings'

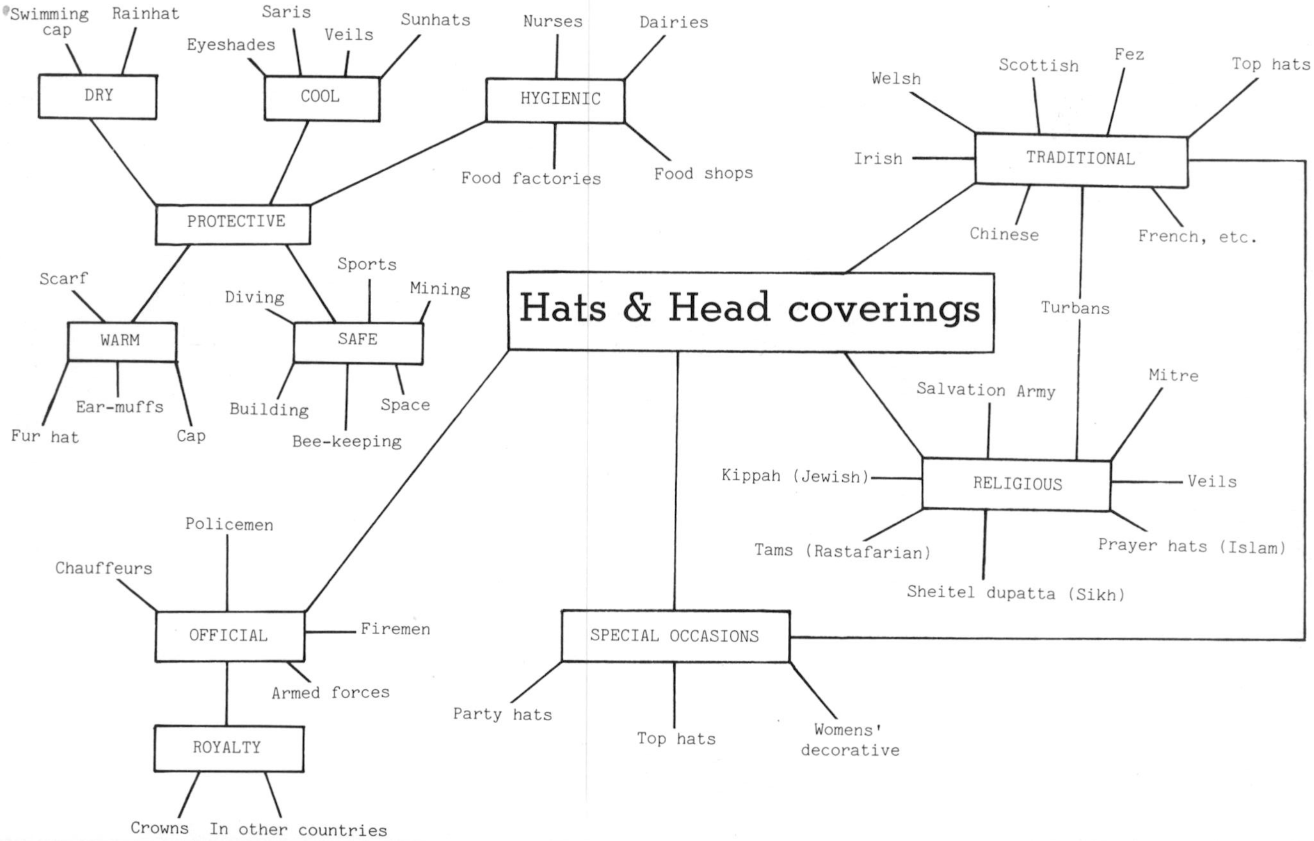

Hats & Head coverings

TRADITIONAL
- Welsh
- Scottish
- Fez
- Top hats
- French, etc.
- Chinese
- Irish
- Turbans

RELIGIOUS
- Mitre
- Veils
- Prayer hats (Islam)
- Sheitel dupatta (Sikh)
- Tams (Rastafarian)
- Kippah (Jewish)
- Salvation Army

HYGIENIC
- Nurses
- Dairies
- Food shops
- Food factories

SPECIAL OCCASIONS
- Womens' decorative
- Top hats
- Party hats

PROTECTIVE
- COOL
  - Eyeshades
  - Saris
  - Veils
  - Sunhats
- DRY
  - Swimming cap
  - Rainhat
- SAFE
  - Sports
  - Mining
  - Space
  - Bee-keeping
  - Building
  - Diving
- WARM
  - Scarf
  - Fur hat
  - Ear-muffs
  - Cap

OFFICIAL
- Firemen
- Armed forces
- Policemen
- Chauffeurs

ROYALTY
- Crowns
- In other countries

Theme 7: Hats and head coverings

Hats and head coverings is an interesting and unusual theme for a topic, which has much potential for multi-cultural work. It is possible to include the ethnic diversity of Britain very naturally by, for example, showing British black and Asian people and others from minority cultures, as well as white Britons, in collages of people wearing hats commonly seen in this country, or by using a similar cultural mix of people to display hats worn in hospitals, factories, mines, and other work places. An illustration of a university 'passing-out' ceremony, showing mortar boards, can well include British people of many cultures.

Moving away from Britain, illustrations and friezes can be produced to show hats and head coverings worn in other countries. A topic on Hats and Head Coverings could select hats for one specific purpose and show how, where, and why variations are found. Thus, Protective Hats or Ceremonial Hats or Religious Hats could be developed in this way.

The topic could select hats from several cultures and look at what they are made of and decorated with. Children could be encouraged to use styles of decoration and patterns from various cultures when they make and draw hats. The permutations within the theme are endless, as are the possibilities for including influences from many cultures.

The basic idea of the theme lends itself to looking at other features of body covering which are common to most of the human race: footwear, males' clothing, females' clothing, unisex clothes, jewellery, face and body decorations, hair and hairstyles, for example.

Teacher aims

* To show the universality of head coverings,
* To discover what factors influence them,
* To incorporate work from most subject areas in the topic.

Pupil objectives

* To enable the children to understand and appreciate:

WHY people wear hats
— to keep warm/cool,

— to keep dry/safe,
— to look nice,
— because of custom,
— for religious purposes,
— for official purposes, uniforms,
— for hygienic purposes.

WHEN people wear hats
— every day,
— at work,
— for special occasions: weddings, festivals, parties,
— for leisure: sports hats, bee-keeping, eye-shields.

WHAT hats people wear
— many different hats are listed under WHERE.

WHERE people wear hats
— in the street: caps, school hats, headscarves, veils, saris, women's and men's street hats,
— at parties: paper hats, fancy hats, joke hats,
— at work: nurses, chefs, miners, builders, sailors, chauffeurs, in factories and food-shops,
— in the sea: swimming hats, divers' helmets,
— in space: space-helmets,
— in hot countries: sun-hats, Arab women's head-coverings, saris, African scarf hats, fezes,
— in cold countries: fur hats, ear muffs, balaclavas, 'Russian' hats,
— in places of worship: turbans, scarves, mitres, Jewish hard hat.

HOW people wear hats
— on head,
— covering hair,
— covering most of face,
— to protect eyes,
— according to fashion.

Hats and head coverings: a breakdown through curriculum subject areas

Reading, writing

Reading and writing are involved in all aspects of topics which are developed through this theme. Many of the points made under other themes will be equally relevant here.

Poetry, rhymes, and story

There are many published stories, poems, and rhymes which can be included if they contain even passing reference to hats and head coverings. Many of the particular favourites of the children and the teacher could be used, with the focus of the topic perhaps encouraging a new look at familiar material.

There are many multi-cultural books which show hats and head coverings from the cultures of Britain, often not as a main focus of the book but still usable in this context.

Children can be encouraged to produce their own stories, poems, and rhymes for reading to each other and to the class, and for making into class books.

Language

Language work can be extended by helping the children to find interesting words to describe the various qualities of hats: shape, colour, texture, size. They could use these words as the basis for creative writing. They could invent names for imaginary hats and real hats could be named in more than one language and script.

Maths

Shape work could be included in the practical side of a Hat topic or in work involving pictures. Symmetry and asymmetry could be introduced in this unusual context, regarding the design, decoration, and shape of hats. Pattern making is easily included when children decorate hats which they have made.

Graphs, sets, measuring and weighing could be included at various points in a Hats and head coverings topic: graphs of the various types of hat in a particular picture; sets of hats made out of various materials; real hats (and heads) can be measured, and the hats weighed. Work on aspects of time could be developed by looking at the various times of day and year at which particular hats are worn.

Science

Science investigations can be drawn from various parts of a Hats and head coverings topic: how protective hats from different cultures do protect; how people would be affected without them; of which materials hats and head coverings are made – wool, cotton, silk, paper, straw, man-made materials; the advantages and disadvantages of these materials.

Geography

Children can be encouraged to discover where particular hats and head coverings come from, and the routes by which they might have arrived in Britain. Other hats, which are not often seen in Britain, may have their countries of origin plotted. The influence of season and climate on the head coverings that are worn in various countries could be studied, as could the same influences on the availability of materials for hats. The type of industry and agriculture in which countries engage, and their economic position, can also be shown to affect people's headgear.

History

Children could study the historical reasons why we see hats and head coverings from so many cultures in Britain. They could project into the future and try to predict the sorts of hat which will be needed then. Tradition and custom in relation to head coverings could be investigated across cultures, as could the historic reasons for using particular materials. Famous hat types from many cultures could be studied.

R.E.

The religious significance of head coverings can be determined, and the attitudes of various faiths towards the covering of heads may be investigated.

Hats and pictures of hats from various faiths can be collected.

Artwork

Children could make head coverings from various cultures and decorate them in the relevant style. They could make collages and friezes featuring hats, ensuring that people from many cultures are portrayed wearing the hats. They could collect and mount pictures of hats from magazines, perhaps making books showing the variety that is possible amongst hats which are intended for one basic purpose.

Music

Music and songs which mention head coverings (not necessarily as the main subject) may be used, perhaps drawing the children's attention to that aspect for the first time. Music connected with occasions for hat-wearing could be played, and the children could be encouraged to write 'hat' songs.

Dance, movement, and drama

Children may create dances for hats which they have made, perhaps linking them with traditional hat dances. They could dramatize or mime occasions when hats are worn: in a street scene, at a sporting event, at a work place, for example.

Hats and head coverings: some resources

Resources from the children

Children will be eager to bring in hats from home. They can search magazines for pictures about the topic; they can provide materials and 'junk' to create their own hats. Family photographs will almost certainly contain some people with hats.

Resources in the local and wider community

Parents and family members may be willing to talk about any hats that they wear for their jobs or for leisure activities. Members of the community who belong to various ethnic groups might be willing to show and talk about hats particular to them. It may be possible to visit workplaces of local occupations which involve hat-wearing.

In 'all-white' areas, the teacher should obtain resources to bring in, to reflect the diversity of modern Britain. However, a surprising amount can often be provided by the children and within the community.

Published resources

The following children's books contain reference to and/or information about the areas indicated:

Abrahams, E. (1986) *Topiwalo the hat maker*, Harmony Publishing Ltd, 14 Silverston Way, Stanmore, Middlesex.
  Picture book for Infants about an Indian village hat-maker who takes his hats to market. Available in Gujerati, Urdu, Punjabi, and Bengali as well as English; tapes also available.
Bennett, O. (1984) *Kikar's Drum*, London: Hamish Hamilton.
  Turbans.
Lawton, C. (1984) *Matza and Bitter Herbs*, London: Hamish Hamilton.
  Jewish *Kippah*.
Lyle, S. (1977) *Pavan is a Sikh*, London: A. & C. Black.
  Turbans.
Mayled, J. (1987) *Religious Dress*, Religious Topic series, Hove, E. Sussex: Wayland.
  Mitre, veil, turban, Islamic prayer hat, Jewish *Kippah*, Sikh *sheitel* and *dupatta*.
Norwood, M. (1986) *I am a Rastafarian*, Franklin Watts.
  Rastafarian tams, Ethiopian scarves.
Scarsbrook, A. and A. (1987) *Junaid in Lahoee*, Beans series, London: A. & C. Black.
  Prayer *topi*.
Solomon, J. *News for Dad*, London: Hamish Hamilton.
  Turbans.
Solomon, J. (1981) *Wedding Day*, London: Hamish Hamilton.
  Traditional head-wear for a Hindu wedding.
(1984) *Phototalk* series, London: ILEA Learning Resources Branch.
  Bathtime with Leanda: African beaded hair.
  Rashan gets Dressed: Sikh patka (topknot), turban.

Work pack

Eid, Multi-Cultural Education Centre, Bishops Road, Bristol BS7 8LS.
  Information on: *topi* – skull caps; *dupatta* or *chuna* – scarf covering
  women's heads; *barunda, paranda* – decorative hair braids.

Illustrations of Hats and head coverings topic

Plate 4.13 Religious hats formed part of a very large topic on Hats, which included uniform and official hats, party hats and so on.

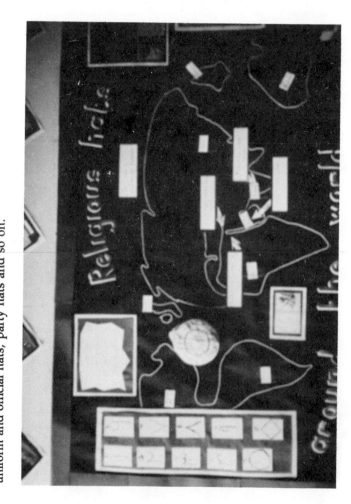

5. Five aspects for personal and social development

Introduction

The five aspects described in this chapter are taken from the Us part of the topic web entitled 'Ourselves' and, for convenience, are dealt with as separate entities here. They are, however, inexorably interlinked and permeate all facets of school life, in both the hidden and open curricula. They are: Self-esteem, Self-awareness, Awareness of others, Relationships, and Thinking and questioning. They form the second, less widely recognized but perhaps most important, side of education for ethnic diversity. The aims of this work are to help children firstly to know, understand, and accept themselves, and then to be able to look outward and value others for their similarities and variations. The work will encourage and develop children's abilities to think and question analytically and critically, so that they can avoid being passive receivers of processed facts.

Teachers and those in training may not find that the concepts which are featured under Aspects are new. Many will have worked on them with classes. What they might find new is consciously thinking through *why* they do as they do, setting long-term aims, and placing continuing emphasis on areas which previously have received only spasmodic attention.

The aims are worked towards through the activities listed under the five aspects, through other similar activities, and through the teacher's realization of the influence of both the latent and open attitudes, behaviour, remarks, and omissions of people in authority. (This point is repeated within the aspects because it is so important and so easy to overlook.) Much of the value of the work lies in the discussion and the exchange of opinions which takes place before, during, and after the activities. Any end-products of written or displayed work take second place to the verbal activity which is generated while working through the activities.

Resources are listed where appropriate. The age ranges for which they are intended vary, but most are adaptable and all will give teachers ideas for work which they can do with their own classes.

Aspect 1: Self-esteem

A sense of self-worth, of the intrinsic value of self, is of vital importance for a realistic acceptance of self and, from there, for the ability to accept and value other people who differ in some way. Feelings of basic insecurity about self lead to the development of an unrealistic, idealistic self-image. This insecure foundation is threatened by any hint of being expected to accept as legitimate, and even welcome, variations of the idealized self. Thus, one of the bedrocks of a personality that is secure enough to embrace variety and change is good self-esteem.

Helping children to develop this is not a one-off job. It involves a process which should start before school and continue throughout education and beyond. Teachers play a very important part in this development not only by being aware of how much value is carried by their behaviour, remarks, omissions, and latent and open attitudes, but also by having a continuous programme of work to help to encourage children's self-valuation.

As with the other areas studied in personal and social development, children gain more from exchanging opinions, discussing, sharing, and valuing, than from producing end-products. Children with very low self-esteem will need considerable positive, and sincere, input which they can *believe*.

Activities to encourage children to realize and acknowledge their own intrinsic value

- Circle games, where the children sit in a circle and, in turn, say their name and something positive about themselves, such as: 'I am David. I am a good reader', 'I am Lisa. I am good at number'; second time around, they say two positive things, and so on.
- A development of the above activity, where the second child repeats what the first child said and adds her/his own statement; the third child repeats what the first two have said and adds her/his own, and so on, round the circle.
- The children sit in a circle and say their names, with a descriptive word first: 'Cheerful Charlie', 'Happy Hussain', 'Friendly Freda'. This could be developed as above.
- As above, but with statements such as 'I am reading Ruth', 'I am painting Paul' which name things that they like doing or are good at.
- The children sit in a double circle, facing each other. One of each pair introduces her/himself and talks positively about her/himself for a minute, then the second child does the same. The inner circle moves on one and the process is repeated.
- The children form pairs and ask each other questions. Each answers them positively and makes an effort to remember what the other says. Two pairs join up and each person introduces her/his partner to the new pair. This could continue up to a maximum of eight children.
- Making 'Pride Plants', where each leaf of the plant contains a positive statement about the child who is making it. These are discussed, admired, and attractively displayed.
- Making 'Positive People', where each child makes a large figure of her/himself, with a body folded concertina-wise, and writes a positive statement about her/himself on each fold. These are discussed and displayed.
- The children make books entitled *About Me*, illustrating good things about themselves.
- The children write positive poems about themselves.
- At the end of each day, the children record something good that they have done.

Another facet of self-esteem is knowing that others value you. Activities to establish this could include:

- Circle games where each child in turn around the circle makes positive statements about the next child.
- Children draw round their hands and decorate the drawings, adding their names. In groups of six, they pass them round. Each child writes a positive statement about the owner of the hand at the tip of one finger and then passes on the drawing. After discussion, the drawings could be displayed in a 'Tree of Friendship'.
- Very similar activities consist of the children drawing round each other's bodies or silhouettes; these outlines are passed round groups, with each person writing in a positive statement about the owner.

Not everything has to be written; a lot can be talked about, painted or drawn, acted out or mimed, and so on.

All of the above activities can be adapted to many ages and should be regarded as a continuous process rather than as isolated activities. They can all be repeated, with deeper effect each time.

Self-esteem: some resources

The best school resource for helping children's self-esteem is the teacher, followed by the general school atmosphere. A teacher who is aware of the influence, both obvious and subtle, that is exerted by authority figures is able to use that influence in a positive way for all the children as individuals. All of the children can feel genuinely valued for the contributions that they make to the class, be it looking after the rabbit, or giving out the milk. They will also be valued in a more subtle way by being noticed by the teacher, by being praised and encouraged. This atmosphere can continue into the school in general by means of the systems of management and discipline that it uses. Authoritarian systems detract from personal development; systems that are more child-centred, which provide children with a say in how the school is run, can give the children real feelings of value.

These less obvious aspects can be of special advantage to the children who are less obviously able, whom it is sometimes hard to praise for doing well in more noticeable areas.

Published resources

The materials mentioned here will often be applicable to the other areas within this chapter. Likewise, resources listed for the other areas may well be of use here.

ACER (Afro-Caribbean Educational Research) Project (1982) *Words and Faces*, London: ILEA Learning Resources Branch.
A pack, with a teacher's book, to help children to develop positive images of themselves and others. Ideas adaptable for primary ages.

ACER (Afro-Caribbean Education Research) Project (1987) *I'm Special Me*, London: ILEA Learning Resources Branch.
A pack for Infants.

Borba, M. and C. (1978) *Self-Esteem: A Classroom Affair*, Winston Press, 430 Oak Grove, Minneapolis, MN55403.
Subtitled '101 ways to help children like themselves', it is full of activities and explains the value of them.

Brandes, D. (1984) *Gamester's Handbook*, London: Hutchinson
Games and activities for all ages. Successor to the following book.

Brandes, D. and Phillips, H. (1977) *Gamester's Handbook*, London: Hutchinson.
Games and activities for all ages, to enhance children's confidence. More games and activities in book above.

Cawfield, J. and Wells, H. (1976) *100 Ways to Enhance Self-Concept in the Classroom*, London: Prentice Hall.
Activities and explanations for them.

Masheder, M. (1988) *Let's Co-operate*, Peace Education Project of the Peace Pledge Union, 6 Endsleigh Street, London WC1 (01-387-5501).
Covers most of the personal and social development areas which are used here, as well as others. Chapter One is on 'A Positive Self-concept'.

Pax Christi (1980) *Winners All (Co-operative Games)*. Available from the Friends Bookshop, Euston Road, London W1.

The following story book, for reading to top Infants or for Junior children, is a sensitive look at how self-esteem can be hurt and how to deal with such situations. It is set in S.E. London and features a black family.

Ashley, B. (1987) *Taller than before*, Clipper Street story, London: Orchard Books.

Illustrations of Self-esteem work

Plate 5.1 Children write down something they are proud of about themselves on leaf-shapes, which then go to make a huge class Pride Plant.

Plate 5.2 Children wrote about something they were proud of on each leaf of their individual plants, for example, being proud of washing up for Mum, or of getting the paper for Dad.

Aspect 2: Self-awareness

Children must have realistic information about themselves, and about their strengths and weaknesses, to enable them to form accurate self-images and achievable goals for themselves. An understanding of both themselves and the fundamental sameness of all people helps them to accept, value, and welcome the peripheral variations within this sameness. This basic similarity is also a feature of much human activity and should be pointed out in other parts of children's work.

Encouraging self-awareness is not an activity that is contained in one piece of work but is a continuing process; activities may be repeated with differing emphasis and deepening learning over many years. Points made previously about the values of talk, and so on, apply equally here.

Activities to encourage self-awareness

- 'Ourselves' is a good starting point and can be pitched at a level to suit the particular children involved. Work on the senses, bodies, organs, and body systems can be done. It should be extended to similarities and variations: height, weight, sex, hair, colour and texture, skin, eyes, foot and hand size, and so on. (See the main topic web, 'Ourselves', on p. 48.) 'Ourselves' is a topic that is often used in schools; its value lies in the attention to detail, the drawing out of similarities and variations, the talking and discussion which is engendered throughout the work.
- Children may be encouraged to draw realistic self-portraits, using mirrors and taking care with colouring. These portraits make interesting class displays and help the children to notice each other.
- Children need to be helped to recognize and acknowledge their feelings, both positive and negative, and to recognize that everybody has similar feelings. There are many activities to encourage this. Children may look at photographs of faces with different expressions and name the feelings; make a frieze of 'Feeling Faces'; make books of 'It makes me happy/sad/angry' about what does make them feel like that; keep a record over a period of time of things that have happened to make them feel different emotions;

make 'Feeling Plants' (Cf. 'Pride Plants' on p. 122); mime feelings; pass facial expressions round a circle or perhaps model the expression of the adjacent person and then pass a different one on to the next person; make books or class pictures 'About me', concentrating on feelings; do the same with 'Likes and Dislikes'.

- A development of this work could lead to a study of personality, image, identity. Children could speculate on these aspects, as illustrated in photographs and pictures of faces, and try to examine themselves in the same way.
- An idea of change can be fostered by encouraging the children to look at how they have developed and how their capabilities have changed; to think of things that they could not do last year but can do now, and of what they hope that they can do in the future; to make (by drawing or writing) 'Life-lines' or 'Life Roadmaps' whereby they illustrate their lives, showing good and bad milestones and, perhaps, predicting the future.

In all of these activities, negative as well as positive feelings require attention. Many of the former can give good insight into individual children's self-images and where they might need sensitive help.

As a realistic awareness of self is the goal, weaknesses as well as strengths must be noticed. Children sometimes place far too much importance on areas of weakness, especially if they have poor self-images, and they can be helped to put these into proportion. Conversely, some children are able to ignore weaknesses that, if noted and acted upon, could develop nicer people. Again, these children can be helped to pay sensible attention to these areas.

Self-awareness: some resources

The children themselves are a major resource here. The depth of their awareness depends quite heavily on the teacher's skill in going beyond superficialities.

Published resources

As these five aspects of personal and social development are so closely interwoven, useful material for this area will be listed in the resources of the others, while material mentioned here will also include some that is useful in the other areas.

ACER (Afro-Caribbean Education Research) Project *Ourselves*, London: ILEA Learning Resources Branch.
   A pack containing activities, teachers' notes, and a resource guide for each of the following themes: Appearance and Personality, Images and Identity, People and Heroes, Home and Family.
Kincaid, D. and Coles, P. (1983) *Read and Do*, Leeds: Arnold-Wheaton.
   Series of eight titles, covering areas such as 'Touch and Feel', 'Taste and Smell', 'Eyes and Looking'; not much different from similar books, but an effort has been made to include illustrations showing various ethnic groups.
Staffordshire County Council LEA (1986) *Multi-Cultural Perspectives in the Primary School*, Staffordshire County Council Education Department.

All schools will have existing resources for looking at 'Ourselves' and these are too numerous to list. Most will serve their purpose, as long as the teacher is aware of the deeper aims of the work and is willing to search out multi-cultural materials, in the form of pictures, posters, and general articles, to supplement the probably mono-cultural nature of the contents.

Illustrations of Self-awareness work

Plate 5.3 Children make a Tree of Life to record significant events –
both happy and sad – in their lives, and to recall how they used to
be.

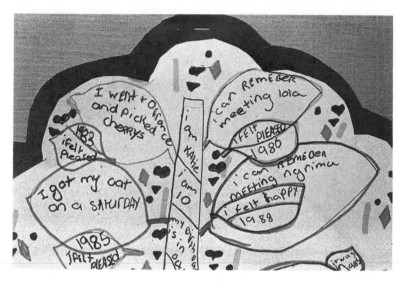

Plate 5.4 This work helped the children to acknowledge and accept
that everybody feels scared sometimes. A neighbouring frieze
illustrated feeling happy.

Aspect 3: Awareness of others

Alongside a developing understanding and valuing of self, children must be able to extend outwards into an understanding of, and sensitivity towards, others. The ability to empathize with other people, to put themselves into others' shoes, must be encouraged and developed through a continuous programme, which deepens as the children mature. Should this area of education be neglected, children are in danger of becoming adults who cannot appreciate other people's points of view and who are unable to recognize the gross inequalities that exist in our society. If these are not at least acknowledged by the next generation, the hope of change is very small.

Discussion is essential; the finished, displayed product does not necessarily reflect the depth of learning that has taken place. Teachers' own, often hidden, attitudes play a part in this area.

Activities to encourage awareness of others

- Some of the activities that are noted under 'Self-esteem' and 'Self-awareness' carry an awareness of others, such as those about 'others valuing us', feelings, similarities and variations.
- Children often do not know the names of people in their own classes. Many of the circle games involve naming oneself and others: a memory game of trying to name everybody in the circle, or of introducing a partner to somebody else, is good here.
- A variety of work can be done to help children to get to know others at school, both children and adults, with whom they will come into either regular or infrequent contact, such as schools meals staff or the school nurse. Introducing people who visit the classroom is a start.
- A 'guess who' game, using unnamed silhouettes, helps children really to observe.
- Playing some of the circle games with closed eyes makes children concentrate on voice variations.
- Identifying others by touch also helps awareness.
- The children sit in a double circle, facing each other. Each

pair takes turns in asking, 'What are you good at?' and then 'What else are you good at?' The inner circle moves on one and the process is repeated. At the end, each child could be asked to remember one thing about some of the children to whom they had spoken.

- Using a 'talking stone' at discussion times: only the child with the stone may speak. This helps children to recognize that others have rights and encourages co-operation in working out how the stone will be passed.
- Explaining how we feel when people 'put us down' or 'build us up' and thus how others feel when we do this. One way is to record incidents of both over a period of time and to discuss them with the class. Another is to make a game where each child has ten unifix cubes in a column; a unifix is taken away for each 'put down' or one is added for each 'build up'. Alternatively each child makes graphs to record these occasions.
- Recognizing when we do positive or negative things to others; making 'I'm sorry' boards and 'I helped' boards.
- Thinking ourselves into other lives: how we would feel and react as babies, old people, imagined people, handicapped people, animals, and so on. Much factual information and experience would be necessary first. This would be gained from children's own lives, visits, stories, television.
- Having lots of stories, songs, poems, pictures, and posters that pick up points of variation in lifestyles, work, religions, age, and appearance, and referring to these as normal features of life.

Awareness of others: some resources

Most of the material in Part II is a potential resource, as it is trying to point outwards from 'Us'. If many ethnically diverse resources, in the widest sense of that word, are used throughout the whole school, children will easily absorb information about other people.

Published resources

All of the children's books that are listed under the various themes in Chapter 4 help towards an awareness of others. See also:

Rosen, M. (1982) *Everybody Here*, London: Bodley Head, in association with Channel 4 Television.
  Based on a Channel 4 magazine programme, this is a well-illustrated collection of stories, activities, songs, and games, which features children from many of the cultures of Britain.

The following are some of the many packs that are useful in this and other areas of personal and social development:

ABC Photo Pack ILEA London: Learning Resources Branch.
  Twenty-six laminated colour photographs of children from a range of cultural backgrounds and a teacher's book with suggestions for activities. The photos are the same as those used in the *ABC Frieze*, also produced by ILEA Learning Resources Branch.
Just Like Us Photographs (1980) London: ILEA Learning Resources Branch.
  A photographic pack about urban children from varied ethnic backgrounds. The teacher's book suggest how the pack might be used: as discussion points, as a basis for writing, and so on.
People Around Us Project Pack, London: A. & C. Black in association with ILEA.
  Unit 1, 'Families', contains photographs, worksheets for photocopying, twelve copies each of two books, and a well thought out teacher's book. It explains the idea of families, starting with the children's own and extending outwards.
Photographs from Bangladesh, London: ILEA Learning Resources Branch.
  Black-and-white photographs and a teacher's book with suggestions for their use.
What's in a Family? (1985), Birmingham: Development Education Centre.
  Black-and-white photographs of many varied British families, plus a teacher's book.

Illustrations of Awareness of others work

Plate 5.5 Looking objectively at Hippies when they were in the news, helped the children to be factually aware of a group of people who form a part of our society.

Plate 5.6 Recognizing class-mates by their silhouettes makes children look carefully at each other, and helps them to focus on people as individuals.

Aspect 4: Relationships

Children need to gain insights into relationships – how they are formed, how they work, how they are broken, and so on – to be able to work happily within society. They have much experience to draw upon, although they will not consciously be aware of it. They have all experienced some form of family relationship, have moved into the wider world of school relationships and friendships, and have varying amounts of experience of relationships within their own communities.

Work on relationships gives children the opportunity and the insight for thinking about how they behave with and react to other people, and how others do so towards them. Cause and effect can be seen to be at work in relationships. Sensitive work in this area helps the children to have some insight into their own, and others', thoughts and actions, and helps them to learn that they can control these to an increasing extent. The aims in this area of study are for the children to achieve not only self-discipline but also the desire and the ability to control their own lives. This obviously involves other people; understanding cause and effect in themselves helps them to do likewise in other people.

As with the other areas highlighted in this chapter, these developments are long term and will continue after schooling has ended. They do need to be encouraged from an early age and built up gradually.

Discussion and sharing are vital elements in the work. The children can gain many insights into their own relationships by listening and contributing.

Activities to encourage children to examine and understand relationships

Looking at:

- What friends are and are not; what they do and do not do.
- Why we like our friends.
- Why we need friends.
- How to make friends: useful strategies, such as offering to share, inviting to play, noticing others.
- How to keep in touch with friends who move or are absent.

- How to keep friends: co-operation, sharing, knowing how far to be influenced.
- Families; over a period of time, drawing out the roles that people play within families.
- The roles that various people play in our own lives.
- The roles we play in other people's lives.
- How people's roles change according to the group or situation in which they are: our mother is our mother, but she is her mother's daughter.
- How individual behaviour affects other people's behaviour towards us: at home, at school, in the community.

Work on relationships can widen out as the children develop. It can encompass areas such as our relationships with our immediate society, with national society, and with the wider world. Recognition, and a growing understanding, of the 'global village' aspect of that world and global interdependence would also fit in here.

All of these activities should be worked through in discussion. They could be extended by making friezes about 'Making Friends', by making individual or class books, by making charts, by having suggestion boards. They would form a good basis for drama and mime. Children could be encouraged to produce some thoughtful written work, including imaginative stories about friends, friendship, and various relationships.

A related activity is looking at games. Most games need friends to play them, and some understanding of relationships to make them work. Children could:

- Make books about playground games, home games, indoor and outdoor games, singing games, ball games, and so on. These could be used as a continuing resource in school.
- Go on to look at world-wide games, the universality of games.
- Learn games from other countries.
- Use the dynamics of actual games to see practical examples of relationships at work.

To look at many of these points, it will be possible to use situations that occur all of the time in schools. Much can be done fairly quickly, but it must be done very frequently, to help the children to get into the habits of analysing situations and of drawing benefits from this analysis.

Relationships: some resources

All of the children will have their own experiences of relationships upon which to draw. Many of the books which they see and read will concern relationships in some way or another. Teachers will find references to the area in much of their resource material; this can be utilized for work on relationships.

Published resources

Some of the items that are listed under Aspect 3 are relevant here, as are parts of *Let's Co-operate* (Masheder, 1986), listed under Aspect 1.

People Around Us Project Pack, London: A. & C. Black in association with ILEA.
Unit 2, 'Friends', contains photographs, worksheets for photocopying, a good teacher's book, a game, and twelve copies of a book in which children from various backgrounds talk about the games that they play.

Resources for games

Some of the multi-cultural children's books, and some of the work packs mentioned on pp. 106 and 129 contain references to games and sometimes instructions for them. For example, *A Day With Ling* shows Chinese chequers, *Pavan is a Sikh* has two Punjabi games in it.

Dunn, O. (compiler) (1978) *Let's Play Asian Children's Games*, Macmillan Southeast Asia with Asian Cultural Centre for UNESCO.
This book, probably best for teacher reference, contains fifty-five games from fifteen Asian countries.
Pendlebury, D. (1986) *Games from Bangladesh and Pakistan.*

Children, their parents, and the local community could all prove to be rich sources of traditional games for inside and outside, for playground, for one, two, or several people.

Illustrations of Relationships

Plate 5.7 Examining the roles and the relationships of people close to us is a first step towards recognizing the relationships within wider society.

Plate 5.8 Helping the children to begin to appreciate world-wide relationships.

Aspect 5: Thinking and questioning

Throughout all of this work, it is necessary to encourage the habits of critical and analytical questioning and thinking. Children are growing up to live in a very complex world, with many options open to them and many factors ready to influence them. While we do not wish to impose our own or other people's ideas on them, we do wish to see them equipped with abilities which will enable them to weigh up the facts that they have; to recognize when they do not have enough facts; to know where to go to find out more; to recognize bias, stereotyping, and prejudice; generally to be in a position to make up their own minds about things. Additional qualities which young people need to be able to function in our world, are being able to think clearly, but not inflexibly; being able to handle varied influences; and being able to take a reasoned, defendable position on important principles.

Children have, from a very young age, questioning, reasoning minds and a sense of fairness and justice. These are qualities that can be seen to be valued and encouraged at school by the way in which the teacher presents work for them.

Children can be challenged to think and follow through their thoughts to a logical conclusion; they can be helped to question, to look at 'facts' with an informed eye. Children respond to being asked consistently to justify statements which they make, to weigh their opinions, to find out more. If they know that their contributions are going to be valued, and that everybody has a chance to speak, the habits of thinking and questioning will be fostered right through school.

Any written or displayed work which shows thinking and questioning will, inevitably, be a very small part of the work that has taken place. Most of the work will be verbal, in discussion, sharing, and finding out. Hearing and thinking about others' opinions on subjects such as gender, resolving conflict and arguments, how old, sick, and handicapped people are treated, whether superficial variations matter, other cultures, will help children to know their own minds, and, indeed, to have minds of their own.

Activities to encourage children's thinking and questioning

- Show that children's opinions are valued by listening to them and acting upon them.
- Plan work so that children need to search out information for themselves.
- Present as many sides of a problem as possible and expect the children to make up their own minds.
- Encourage the children to work in groups, so that they develop skills in evaluating contributions towards a common aim.
- Use debating and class discussion, making sure that all children feel able to contribute.
- Give the children experiences of democratic decision making: where to go on class trips, how limited resources will be used fairly, how class chores shall be shared, and so on.
- Use questioning in class displays, so that children interact with them, rather than passively observing them. Change the questions and displays frequently in order to maintain interest.

Illustrations of Thinking and questioning work

Plate 5.9 The children
have used a story book
to see how readily we fit
people into pre-conceived
stereotypes, and to see
how wrong these can be.
(Gray, W. and Forman,
M: 1985 *I'll take you to
Mrs Cole*, London,
Anderson Press.)

Plate 5.10 This piece of
writing was done after
a class discussion
about 'normality'.

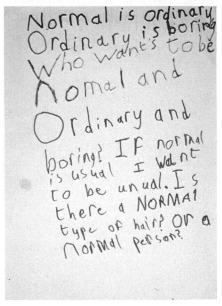

6. Three interweaving strands

Introduction

The three areas which are dealt with in this chapter – language diversity, ethnic diversity within maths, and ethnic diversity around school – have been singled out not only because they are constituent parts of the work in Chapters 4 and 5 but also because they may be treated as discrete units in their own right.

Language diversity and diversity within maths may be achieved in individual classrooms but, like all of the other areas, they are far more effective if they derive from a policy that is thought out and acted upon by the whole school.

Strand 3, ethnic diversity around school, obviously cannot be effectively accomplished by just one or two individuals. Since it also encompasses rather different territory to the other two strands, an additional introductory piece has been included to indicate what these different factors are.

Each of the three strands includes examples of Teacher aims and of Pupil objectives, which detail some of the learning goals that children should be able to achieve. Ideas follow for ways and means of achieving these goals and, finally, there are lists of sources of materials and resources.

Strand 1: Language diversity

In this as in the other areas, much of the value for children lies in the talking, discussion, and discovery which take place during their work. For language diversity to have meaning for the children, it must be included in purposeful activities and

not be 'added on' by the teacher to finished displays or, out
of context, to other pieces of work. The teacher should
consider language diversity during the planning of class work,
so that it forms one of the strands that is interwoven through
all of the children's work.

Care should be taken when trying to encourage bi-lingual
and bi-dialectual children to contribute in their mother
tongues. Children are easily embarrassed if they are made to
feel different. Often an indirect approach, which arises from
meaningful situations such as picking up on chance words that
are used, or else a more general starting point, which
encourages contributions from all of the children, is more
acceptable than direct requests for words.

Teacher aims

* To illustrate the universality of language,
* To look at the variety within languages,
* To bring language diversity into all the work of the children.

Pupil objectives

* To enable the children to:
— become less insular and to develop a broader outlook,
— realize that there is not just one correct response in
  language, as in other areas,
— gain an insight into the richness of the world's languages,
— recognize and value the variety and richness of dialects and
  accents,
— develop an added interest in their own language,
— to become aware that languages other than English are
  commonly spoken and read in Britain and not just in other
  countries,
— learn to value other people's skills in languages, particularly
  bi-lingual classmates,
— gain an insight into the status of various languages, dialects
  and accents.

Activities and strategies to encourage language diversity

- Having meaningful and familiar books in more than one language around the class and school, as a normal resource.
- Having tapes of familiar stories in other languages, whether or not there are speakers of that language at school.
- Having story sessions in other languages, using familiar, well-prepared stories.
- Using the home languages of bi-lingual or non-English speaking pupils around the school and in communications with parents.
- Finding out what languages/accents/dialects are known about/used/learned in the class/school/local community. Children could conduct a survey, make graphs to plot the results, use maps to see from where the language, etc. originated; work could extend into finding out why the languages are known: by immigration, holidays, relatives, examination work, and so on.

Working through specific language topics:

- Look at various alphabets, speculating on how they came to be written, why they differ, why a need was felt for them; the countries in which they are used could be studied, the numbers of people using them discovered, and graphs and sets made; their differing and similar sounds could be examined, and the varying shapes could be used in artwork.
- Scripts and languages could be studied in the same way, with examples in common use found: newspapers, stamps, instructions on articles, etc.
- Varying number systems could be used in the same way.
- Extending this work by: looking at other ways to communicate: animal and bird language; 'chemical' language; body language: human, animal, insect; codes: Morse, flag and secret signs; signals, Braille; Moon.
- Looking at names: what they mean; how they are given: nicknames, pet names, 'given' names; changing names; 'stage' names; writing them in various scripts; similar names in various languages and dialects; other naming systems; pattern-making with names, collage work; names beginning with the same letter; sets and graphs of names; names for

articles (clothes, food, etc.) in more than one language.

- Looking into various ways of saying 'Mum', 'Dad'; of saying hello and welcome in more than one language; names for body parts, toys.
- Finding universal themes in songs, rhymes, games, stories.

Language diversity: some resources

Resources from the children

The children will often have some knowledge of languages other than English, which may be utilized in various ways.

They may well have examples of various languages at home: on postcards, on food from other countries, on stamps, in newspapers, and so on.

Some children will have tapes and records which illustrate accents and dialects.

Resources in the local and wider community

Parents, staff, and local people may provide a rich source of languages, dialects and accents. They may be willing to come to talk to the children or perhaps to contribute their voices on a tape. Some of them might be encouraged to come to school to read stories to the children.

Local shops will probably have examples of various languages: on food packages, in newspapers and magazines, on labels and instructions. Many small corner shops are run by people of Asian origin and would be a rich source of language diversity which is very accessible and meaningful to the children.

Radio and television can be used to illustrate languages, dialects, and accents which cannot be found locally.

Published resources

Teachers' resources and reference books

Gregory, A. and Woolard, N. (eds) (1984) *Looking into Language*, Support Service for Language and Intercultural Education, Lydford Road, Reading, Berkshire. Also published by Trentham Books.

Language orientated projects used in schools.

Hawkins, E. (ed.) (1985) *Awareness of Language*, Cambridge: Cambridge University Press.
Booklets covering aspects of language – language for various purposes, first and second language learning, spoken and written language, non-verbal communication – and suggestions for practical use.

Houlton, D. (1985) *All our Languages*, London: Schools Council/Edward Arnold.
Ideas for language diversity. Has good resource list and addresses.

Katzner, K. (1977) *Languages of the World*, London: Routledge & Kegan Paul.
Pages of sample scripts in numerous languages, plus a rather technical categorization of languages.

Raleigh, M. *The Languages Book*, London: ILEA English Centre, Ebury Bridge, Sutherland Street, London SW1.
Practical suggestions for encouraging older children to think about language.

(1984) *The Children's Language Project*, London: Philograph for the University of London Institute of Education.
Teacher's handbook and workcards for Juniors on language at home, at school, around us, near and far.

Children's books

Familiar children's stories are increasingly available in languages other than English. Requests to publishers for more translated books will help to indicate that there is an increasing demand for them.

Language and Writing, Topic series, Hove, E. Sussex: Wayland.
Aimed at 8–12 year olds, but could be adapted.

Scripts and alphabets

Newspapers, magazines, comics, and instructions in languages other than English are fairly easy to obtain.

Examples of various scripts can be found in the following children's books:

Bennett, O. (1983)*Turkish Afternoon*, London: Hamish Hamilton.
Contains some Turkish words.

Knapp, C. (1979) *Shimon, Leah, and Benjamin*, London: A. & C. Black.
Hebrew script.

Lawton, C. (1984) *Matza and Bitter Herbs*, London: Hamish Hamilton.
Hebrew script.

Lyle, S. (1977) *Pavan is a Sikh*, London: A. & C. Black.
Punjabi script.
McCarty, N. (1977) *Rebecca is a Cypriot*, London: A. & C. Black.
Shows a Greek newspaper.
Norwood, M. (1986) *I am a Rastafarian*, London: Franklin Watts.
Amharic (Ethiopian) script.
Tsow, M. (1982) *A Day With Ling*, London: Hamish Hamilton.
Painting Chinese script.

The following packs contain scripts as indicated:

Chinese New Year, Multi-Cultural Education Centre, Bishop Road, Bristol BS7 8LS.
Some Mandarin script, and numbers.
Diwali, Minority Groups Support Service, Southfields Old School, South Street, Hillfields, Coventry CU1 5EJ.
'Happy Diwali' in Gujerati, Hindi, Punjabi.
Eid, Multi-Cultural Education Centre, Bishops Road, Bristol BS7 8LS.
Urdu script and numbers.

Posters illustrating several Asian scripts are available from Soma Books, 38 Kennington Lane, London SE11.

The Nottingham Educational Supplies catalogue contains charts and posters in several languages, and also some alphabet charts in Asian scripts; available from Ludlow Hill Road, West Bridgford, Nottingham NG2 6HD.

Illustration of Language diversity work

Plate 6.1 Naming body parts in several languages highlights our human commonality within the wide diversity of words for our common features. (Including a transliteration for unfamiliar scripts would make them more accessible to English speakers.)

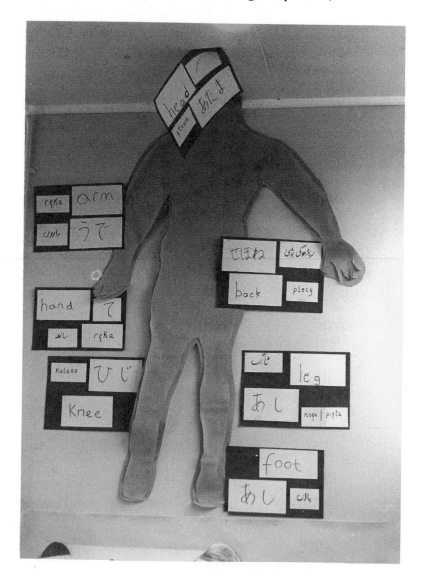

Strand 2: Ethnic diversity within maths

Many teachers are hesitant about including mathematical influences from other cultures in the work that the children do because they feel that they themselves have neither enough knowledge about them nor enough resources. Both of these areas can be built up gradually so that, on the second occasion when a subject is covered, a framework of knowledge, experience, and resources is already in place.

Teaching aid firms and book publishers are more likely to produce resources if they know that there is a demand for them, so teachers must make known (repeatedly if necessary) their multi-cultural mathematics requirements.

Ethnic diversity within maths can be included in many subtle ways. These need not be mentioned continually but do have an effect because of their very existence. More noticeable methods can also be used. Perhaps the most lasting results are achieved by a mixture of both approaches.

Teacher aims

* To illustrate the universality of maths,
* To illustrate the variety within that universality,
* To bring the diversity within maths into all areas of the work of the class.

Pupil objectives

* To enable the children to:
— become less insular and to develop a broader outlook,
— recognize and value the contributions of many peoples to our knowledge of maths,
— gain an insight into the similarities of number systems and methods,
— gain experience of the fascinating applications of maths through many cultures,
— 'see' maths within many meaningful situations rather than as a subject unconnected with real life.

Activities and strategies to encourage ethnic diversity within maths

Introducing diverse material into topics by bringing in:

- Various money systems, when money is being looked at.
- How seasons vary with geographical position.
- How time varies also: the effect of the International Date Line, 'local time'.
- How daylight varies: Arctic night, midnight sun, lack of twilight in tropics.
- Varied calendars and time cycles.
- Various ways of calculating age: some cultures consider children to be a year old at birth.
- Various number systems; playing games in them.
- Varying ways of writing numbers.
- Stamps from lots of countries.

Within topics with multi-cultural content:

- Use multi-cultural material for graphs, sets, mapping: various languages, various building materials, countries to which we have travelled, countries from which relatives come etc.
- Much material within personal and social development lends itself to this: eye colour, hair colour, families, likes and dislikes, etc.

Specifically multi-cultural topics:

- Any area which is specifically studied across cultures: number systems, historic development of number, geometry, naming days, months, symmetry as developed through art forms, decorations, embroidery.

In general:

- Use varied skin tones, facial features, hairstyles, and dress in home-made teaching aids and materials, number cards, counting cards, pictorial 'sums'.
- Find commercial materials which reflect the cultures of Britain.

- Look out for and collect pictures and materials which can be used in maths and which are not 'white': examples of shape, pattern, symmetry, geometry, from other cultures; pasta, pulses for weighing. Talk about the resources so that children absorb knowledge about them.
- Collect various methods of doing the same thing, let the children know that there is not one right way: for example, the abacus for calculating, Asian and Chinese methods of weighing goods by balancing, various ways of telling the time.

Ethnic diversity within maths: some resources

Resources from the children

The children may have experiences and memories of encountering various number and money systems, or of 'losing' or 'gaining' an hour. Some may have experienced different daylight lengths or have knowledge of calendars from other cultures.

Children may have money from other countries or stamps that show varying number scripts, which they can bring to school.

Resources from the local and wider community

Parents, staff, and local people might have knowledge of and articles from, say, varying number systems, which they may be willing to share. If there are shops nearby (a Chinese take-away, an Asian corner ship), it might be possible to borrow calendars and to obtain examples of number scripts. A local bank may be willing to provide coins from various countries, an example of an International Money Order, and so on. Local shops, parents, and staff may well have examples of patterns from other countries: in embroidery, in wall hangings, on cards, on decorations. Stamps from other countries might be available from local people's collections.

Published resources

The following will provide some information and resources

which teachers can adapt and use in the classroom:

Bovett, A. (1983) Maths: A Universal Language, *Multicultural Teaching* I(3), Summer.

Craft, A. and Bardell, G. (eds) (1984) *Curriculum Opportunities in a Multi-cultural Society*, London: Harper & Row.
    Has a section on multi-ethnic maths, including patterns and counting methods.

MacLeod-Brundenell, I. (1986) *Cross-cultural Art Booklets*, Nottingham: Nottingham Educational Supplies.
    The booklet on 'Design' contains many examples which can be used in areas of maths: shape, symmetry, grids, patterns, and so on. The booklet dealing with 'Clay' also has some pattern sources which can be adapted.

Peterborough Centre for Multi-Cultural Education *Magic Squares*, Peterborough Centre for Multi-Cultural Education, 165a Cromwell Road, Peterborough PE1 2EL.
    An ancient Chinese grid game.

Peterborough Centre for Multi-Cultural Education *Number 1–10*, Peterborough Centre for Multi-Cultural Education, 165a Cromwell Road, Peterborough PE1 2EL.
    Numbers 1–10 in Urdu, Bengali, Punjabi, Gujerati.

Wiltshire Education Authority (1988) *Mathematics for All*, Trowbridge: Wiltshire Education Authority, County Hall, Trowbridge.
    This book details material that was used in 'Multi-Cultural Maths Weeks' in Wiltshire. It includes work on number systems, tangrams, Hindu dance, magic squares, and many other areas.

Zaslavsky, C. (1979) *Africa Counts: Number and Pattern in African Culture*, Lawrence Hill, New Youth (from Third World Publications, 151 Stratford Road, Birmingham B11 1RD).
    A reference book with material on number patterns and games, hand signs, and counting aids from various parts of Africa.

Zaslavsky, C. (1980) *Count On Your Fingers, African Style*, New York: Thomas Y. Crowell (available from Harper & Row, London).
    A book for young children, which shows the finger counting of several African peoples, and their words for numbers.

Zaslavsky, C. (1982) *Tic-Tac-Toe and Other Three-in-a-Row Games from Ancient Egypt to the Modern Computer*, New York: Thomas Y. Crowell (available from Harper and Row, London).
    Aimed at junior or lower secondary children, the material is adaptable. Looks at world-wide variations of noughts and crosses.

'Festival Packs' from Multi-cultural Resource Centres

Many of these and other similar packs will contain mathematical references amongst the other information. It is well worth going through material which is already in school and collecting these chance pieces of information. Details of a few of the packs are listed as examples:

Chinese New Year, Multi-Cultural Education Centre, Bishops Road, Bristol BS7 8LS.
Contains examples of some numbers and details of the twelve-year calendar.
Diwali, Minority Groups Support Service, Southfields Old School, South Street, Hillfields, Coventry CU1 5EJ.
Examples of rangoli and alpana floor patterns.
Eid, Multi-Cultural Education Centre, Bishops Road, Bristol BS7 8LS.
Has some mehndi patterns, Islamic geometric patterns, and Urdu numbers.
(*Rangoli*, *alpana*, *mandala*, and *mehndi* are some of the names for traditional Asian patterns, which are often symmetrical and very often based on geometric shapes. Amongst other things, they can be used as tracing patterns for very young children.)

Many of the newer 'multi-cultural' children's books, which are now available, will contain references to mathematical areas amongst the other information. They can provide useful supplementary resources. Books about ancient and modern cultures will often have illustrations of geometric or symmetric patterns which can be used. Fascinating examples of shape and symmetry can be found in some embroidery books and may be adapted for use in schools.

The catalogues of the Educational Suppliers such as Nottingham and ILEA, are beginning to include number material which uses other number systems. Requests to the companies for more multi-cultural maths material would help to establish the demand for it and encourage them to supply that demand.

Inner London Education Authority (1985) *Everyone Counts*, London: ILEA Learning Resources Branch, 275 Kennington Lane, London SE11 5QZ, tel. 01-735-8202.
Subtitled 'Looking for bias and insensitivity in primary mathematics materials', this covers a wide range of areas, including cultural bias and insensitivity. The reasoning behind the contents can equally be applied to any school materials.

Illustrations of Ethnically diverse maths work

Plate 6.2 These children are gaining practical experience of the common purposes of number scripts, by using various scripts for their measuring work.

Plate 6.3 Tangrams were used as one of many examples when the children were looking at squares in their shape work.

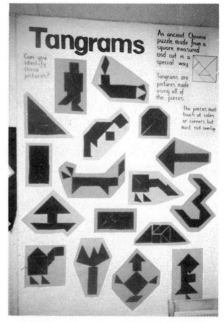

Strand 3: Ethnic diversity around school

Major considerations

To be seen to be ethnically diverse and to care about equality, as opposed to merely paying lip-service, a school must make an effort to ensure that its staff – head, teachers, ancillaries, caretaker, kitchen staff, cleaners – are drawn from as many cultures as possible. This may not be easy in some 'all-white' areas but it is not impossible; it is certainly possible for much of Britain. To carry out a policy of employing a diverse staff, a school must be able to convince its own parents and its governing body of the desirability of such a move, and may well have to press the point with its local education authority. Although in some areas this may seem a pointless operation, the *status quo* will not change by itself; the more that schools are seen to be pressing for such policies, the more that reluctant LEAs will feel the need to change. However, obtaining general agreement to an 'equal opportunities' policy at local authority level is not enough; both strategies to carry it out and a monitoring system to plot its effectiveness are essential.

It is equally important that minority cultures are represented throughout the whole staffing structure of the school and are not restricted to low-status positions.

For a school to be committed to ethnic diversity and to equality within the school, the staff need to have thought out their attitudes towards and strategies for multi-cultural and anti-racist education. They must include a policy for dealing with racist remarks and behaviour. 'All-white' schools will often protest that they have no such incidents but, unfortunately,they are nearly always present and must be dealt with consistently, each time they occur, by all staff. The fact that there may be few or no black, Asian, or other minority culture pupils in the school is irrelevant. To ignore illustrations of prejudice amongst pupils (and amongst some of the adults in schools) is to condone them and to give them status by omitting to take positive action against them.

Much has been written elsewhere on both of these areas. Information about how to reach a school policy on staffing and racist behaviour may be found in several of the books listed in Part 1, Chapter 2.

Another area that can positively demonstrate a school's

attitude towards ethnic diversity is the effort that is put into encouraging the parents of all pupils to be involved with the life of the school. Some teachers may say that parents from ethnic minorities are too shy/have no time/are not interested/ would be embarrassed because there is only one such British family, but these reasons are often propounded to cover the teachers' own diffidence at approaching parents who perhaps do not speak much English. It does need an effort on the part of the teachers, because many parents *are* shy or have little time, but this applies to white parents as well as to minority culture parents. Children are very quick to sense a class and/or culture barrier by means of the parents who are not represented amongst those who help in school, or the type of job which the parents who are in school are asked to do. There are few parents, of any culture, who are unwilling to help in some way or another, if they are asked sensitively. Teachers must ensure that ethnic minority parents, as well as white parents, are asked to help over the full range of jobs.

Parents from minority cultures have the advantage of being able to help in the areas of their culture, by telling stories in their mother tongue, by contributing their real experiences, and by just being in school.

Teacher aims

* To reflect the present-day multi-cultural society of Britain throughout the school,
* To bring examples of the wider world into the children's normal experiences and environment,
* To integrate the above into the life of the school rather than have them as isolated items in the curriculum.

Pupil objectives

* To enable the children to:
— widen their outlook, their ideas and concepts of what Britain is today,
— look outwards into the world with interest rather than with suspicion,
— enjoy and accept the variety that is available within many cultures rather than to stick rigidly to one, supposedly

'right' way,
— absorb these influences naturally rather than experiencing them as 'spectacles',
— value other people and cultures.

Activities and strategies to encourage ethnic diversity around school

- Start to buy and display books that are ethnically diverse, especially those that bring diversity into 'ordinary' themes.
- Collect and present, as part of the normal displays, posters that feature people with varied skin tones, hair types, facial features, and clothing.
- Ensure that children have knowledge about and access to varied tones for painting people in all of their pictures and friezes and not just in topics on Africa or India.
- Obtain fabrics from other cultures to use for drapes (wall hangings, room dividers, etc.) and as backgrounds for displays.
- Include clothes from other cultures for 'dressing up', preferably real clothes and not specially bought 'costumes'.
- Include artefacts from other cultures in the Home Corner, not for special occasions but alongside the frying-pan and knives and forks.
- Include pictures, art, and artefacts from other cultures around the school.
- Label appropriate items and give some background information.
- Use languages other than English around the school as a matter of course. Do not use only those languages that are mother tongues of the children in the school.
- Make sure that mother tongue languages are used in notices, labels, and communications with parents.
- Select new material from the educational catalogues with an eye for varied skin tones, facial features, etc. in workcards, jigsaws, games, and dolls.
- Vary the content of home-made teaching aids to include Britons of black, Asian, and other cultures as well as white Britons.
- Include patterns from other cultures in tracing cards.
- Keep ethnic diversity in mind for all aspects of school, latent as well as open.

- Try to encourage the meals service to include a wide variety of dishes for the children, many of whom will have experienced the dishes at home.

Multi-cultural books, posters, displays, and artefacts, which are around the school and are a normal part of school life, help to make ethnic diversity an accepted reality, replacing what is frequently an ethnocentric, mono-cultural (and sometimes xenophobic and racist) outlook on life.

Ethnic diversity around school: some resources

Resources from the children

Children may be willing to bring articles from other cultures to school, for general display rather than as 'special' exhibits. (The school gives value to things, in the children's eyes, just be showing an interest in them.) Children from minority British cultures may be willing to contribute everyday articles from their homes, again not as spectacles but as part of school life. Children will have holiday experiences to share of being impressed by certain aspect of other cultures.

Resources from the local and wider community

Parents, staff, and local people may well be willing to loan items, such as pictures, posters, artefacts, clothing, fabrics, books, to be generally displayed in school. Local shops may have goods for sale from other cultures which the school could use. They may also have display posters which they no longer require.

Many schools are in or are reasonably near a large city or town, in which there are more and more 'ethnic' areas or shops where everyday items can be purchased.

There is an increasing number of mail-order catalogues, such as those from Oxfam or Traidcraft, which include articles from other countries.

Some schools encourage teachers, helpers, and others to bring back articles from holiday for the school. These are *not* souvenirs but are small, real items from other cultures: sari lengths, domestic articles, games, toys, newspapers, comics, and well-known books. An upper price limit is set. A good collection can be built up in this way.

Published resources

Many of the Educational Suppliers' catalogues have an increasing amount of suitable material available, although it is necessary to search through the catalogues to find it. Nottingham Educational Supplies, Galt, and E.J. Arnold are examples of firms who are including some ethnically diverse materials.

It is well worth obtaining the ILEA catalogue from Learning Resources Branch, 275 Kennington Lane, London SE11 5QZ, tel: 01-735-8202. (Please note that the address for this catalogue seems to change frequently.)

A new supplier of multi-cultural educational equipment is Unity Learning Foundation, 10 Barley Mow Passage, London W4 4PH, tel: 01-994-6477. The catalogue includes dolls, glove puppets, clothes, musical instruments, jigsaws. Some items that were previously available through Lambeth Toys are included in the catalogue.

The Support team for bi-lingual under fives, (CUES), Lilian Bayliss School, Lawn Lane, Vauxhall, London SW8, tel: 01-735-0656, produces a resource list which includes addresses for home corner materials, crafts, food, books, cards, posters, dolls, musical instruments, as well as addresses for other useful information.

There are also a number of highly useful school and LEA policy documents which detail various aspects of whole school policies. These are discussed and described briefly in Part 1, Chapter 2.

Illustrations of Ethnic diversity around school

Plate 6.4
Artefacts from
other cultures,
including dolls,
need to be seen
as a normal
part of the
school
environment,
and not as
articles to be
brought out
only for
'special'
occasions.

Plate 6.5 Decorations, pictures and hangings from many cultures were displayed in this school. The class name, written in two scripts, gives subtle recognition of the diversity of world languages.

References and bibliography

Adams, C., Reyersbach, A., and Bourdillon, H. (1986) *Implementing the ILEA's anti-sexist policy: a guide for schools*, London: ILEA Equal Opportunities Inspectorate.

Anti-Racist Teacher Network (1988) *Anti-Racist Teacher Education: Permeation: The Road to Nowhere*, Glasgow: ARTEN/Jordanhill College of Education, Glasgow G13 1PP. Or Jane Lane, Commission for Racial Equality, Elliot House, 10–12 Allington Street, London SW1E 5EH.

Arora, R. and Duncan, C. (1986) *Multi-cultural Education Towards Good Practice*, London: Routledge and Kegan Paul.

Assistant Masters and Mistresses Association (1982) *Our Multi-Cultural Society: The Educational Response*, London: Assistant Masters and Mistresses Association (AMMA).

Ball, S. (1986) *Education*, London: Longman.

Benn, C. and the Socialist Teachers Alliance (1988) 'A Socialist Education Policy', *Interlink*, Spring.

Berkshire Local Education Authority (1983) *Policy Statement on Racial Equality and Justice*, Reading: Berkshire County Council.

Bewbush First School (1988) *Bewbush First School Equal Opportunities Policy*, Crawley: Bewbush First School, Dorsten Square, Crawley, West Sussex.

Bowles, H. and Gintis, S. (1976) *Schooling in Capitalist America: Educational Reform and the Contradictions of Economic Life*, London: Routledge and Kegan Paul.

Brandt, G.L. (1986) *The Realization of Anti-Racist Teaching*, London: Falmer Press.

Brent (London Borough) (1983) *Education for a Multicultural Democracy*, Books 1 and 2, London: London Borough of Brent Education Committee.

Bullivant, B. (1986) 'Towards Radical Multiculturalism: Resolving Tensions in Curriculum and Educational Planning', in S. Modgil *et al.* (eds) *Multicultural Education: the Interminable Debate*, London: Falmer Press.

Chapman, K. (1986) *Sociology of Schools*, London: Tavistock.

Cohen, L. and Cohen, A. (eds) (1986) *Multi-Cultural Education: A Source Book for Teachers*, London: Harper and Row.

Cohen, P. and Bains, H.S. (1988) *Multi-Racist Britain: New Directions in Theory and Practice*, Basingstoke: Macmillan Education.

Cole, M. (1986) 'Teaching and Learning about Racism: A Critique of Multicultural Education in Britain', in S. Modgil *et al.* (eds) *Multicultural Education: The Interminable Debate*, London: Falmer Press.

Cole, M. (ed.) (1989) *The Social Contexts of Schooling*, London: Falmer Press.

Cole, M. (ed.) (1989) *Education for Equality: Some Guidelines for Good Practice*, London: Routledge.

Commission for Racial Equality (1985) *Swann: A response from the Commission for Racial Equality*, London: Commission for Racial Equality (CRE).

Commission for Racial Equality (1988) *Annual Report*, London: Commission for Racial Equality (CRE).

Commission for Racial Equality (1988) *Learning in Terror: A survey of racial harassment in schools and colleges*, London: Commission for Racial Equality (CRE).

Corrigan, P. (1979) *Schooling the Smash Street Kids*, London: Macmillan.

Council for National Academic Awards (1984) *Multi-Cultural Education: Discussion Paper*, London: Council for National Academic Awards (CNAA).

Craft, M. (1984) *Education and Cultural Pluralism*, London: Falmer Press.

Department of Education and Science (1982) *The New Teacher in School: A Survey by HM Inspectors in England and Wales 1981*, London: Her Majesty's Stationery Office.

Department of Education and Science (1984) *Initial Teacher Training: Approval of Courses*, Circular 3/84, London: Her Majesty's Stationery Office.

Department of Education and Science (1988) *Secondary Schools: An Appraisal by HMI*, London: Her Majesty's Stationery Office.

Department of Education and Science (1988) *The New Teacher in School: A Survey by HM Inspectors in England and Wales 1987* London: Her Majesty's Stationery Office.

Department of Education and Science (1989) *Science in the National Curriculum*, London: Her Majesty's Stationery Office.

Department of Education and Science (1989) *Mathematics in the National Curriculum*, London: Her Majesty's Stationery Office.

Department of Education and Science (1989) *The National Curriculum: From Policy to Practice*, London: Her Majesty's Stationery Office.

East Sussex County Council (1988) *Multicultural Education Policy and Support*, Lewes: East Sussex County Council.

Flew, A. (1986) 'Education Against Racism', in D. O'Keefe (ed.) *The Wayward Curriculum: A Cause for Parents' Concern*, London: Social Affairs Unit.

Gaine, C. (1987) *No Problem Here: A Practical Approach to Education and 'Race' in White Schools*, London: Hutchinson.

Gaine, C. (1989) *Getting Equal Opportunities Policies*, London: Routledge.

Gaine, C. and Pearce, L. (1988) *Anti-Racist Education in White Areas*, NAME Conference Report, Walsall National: Anti-Racist Movement in Education. (Available from Chris Gaine, West Sussex Institute of Higher Education, Bognor Regis, West Sussex.)

German, G. (1988) Letter in *Times Educational Supplement*, 22 July.

Giroux, H.A. (1983) *Theory and Resistance in Education: A Pedagogy for the Opposition*, London: Heinemann.

Giroux, H.A. (1986) *Education Under Siege*, London: Routledge and Kegan Paul.

Gordon, P. (1989) 'The New Educational Right', *Race and Immigration* no. 224, April, London: Runnymede Trust.

Gordon, P. and Newnham, A. (1986) *Different Worlds: Racism and Discrimination in Britain*, 2nd edn, London: Runnymede Trust.

Greater London Action for Race Equality (GLARE) (1989) 'Race Equality and the Education Reform Act', Room 312, Southbank House, Black Prince Road, London SE1 7SJ.

Gurnah, A. (1987) 'Gatekeepers and Caretakers: Swann, Scarman, and the Social Policy of Containment', in B. Troyna (ed.) *Racial Inequality in Education*, London: Tavistock.

Haralambos, M. and Heald, R. (1985) *Sociology: Themes and Perspectives*, London: University Tutorial Press.

Hatcher, R. (1987) '"Race" and Education: two perspectives for change', in B. Troyna (ed.) *Racial Inequality in Education*, London: Tavistock.

Hatcher, R. and Shallice, J. (1983) 'The Politics of anti-racist education', *Multiracial Education* 12 (1). Quoted in S. Modgil *et al.* (eds) (1986) *Multi-Cultural Education: The Interminable Debate*, London: Falmer Press, Chap. 1.

Hill, D. (1989) *The Charge of the Right Brigade: the Radical Right's Assault on Teacher Education*, 75 Alkham Road, London N16 6XF.

Hillgate Group (1987) *The Reform of British Education – from principles to practice*, London: The Claridge Press.

Hillgate Group (1989) *Learning to Teach*, London: The Claridge Press.

Honeyford, R. (1988) Letter in *Times Educational Supplement*, 22 July.

Inner London Education Authority (1982) *Anti-Racist School Policies*, London: ILEA, Multi-Ethnic Inspectorate, room 468, County Hall, London SE1 7AB.

Inner London Education Authority (1983) *Race, Sex and Class 1. Achievement in Schools*, London: ILEA, Multi-Ethnic Inspectorate.

Inner London Education Authority (1983) *Race, Sex and Class 2. Multi-Ethnic Education in Schools*, London: ILEA, Multi-Ethnic Inspectorate.

Inner London Education Authority (1983) *Race, Sex and Class 3. A Policy for Equality: Race*, London: ILEA Multi-Ethnic Inspectorate.

Inner London Education Authority (1983) *Race, Sex and Class 4. Anti-Racist Statement and Guidelines*, London: ILEA Multi-Ethnic Inspectorate.

Inner London Education Authority (1983) *Race, Sex and Class 5. Multi-Ethnic Education in Further, Higher and Community Education*, London: ILEA Multi-Ethnic Inspectorate.

Inner London Education Authority (1984) *Education in a Multi-Ethnic Society: The Primary School*, London: ILEA Multi-Ethnic Inspectorate.

Inner London Education Authority (1984) *Committee on the Curriculum and Organisation of Secondary Schools – Improving Secondary Schools: Report of the Committee on the Curriculum and Organisation of Secondary Schools*, chaired by David Hargreaves, London: ILEA. Known as the 'Hargreaves Report'.

Inner London Education Authority (1985) *Committee on Primary Education – Improving Primary Schools: Report of the Committee on Primary Education*, chaired by Norman Thomas, London: ILEA. Known as the 'Thomas Report'.

Interlink (Journal of the Conference of Socialist Economists and of the Socialist Society), London: 9 Poland Street, London W1.

Jeffcoate, R. (1984) *Ethnic Minorities and Education*, London: Harper and Row.

Klein, G. (1985) *Reading into Racism: Bias in Children's Literature and Learning Materials*, London: Routledge and Kegan Paul.

Lynch, J. (1986) *Multi-Cultural Education: Principles and Practice*, London: Routledge and Kegan Paul.

Macdonald, I. (1988) *The Macdonald Inquiry into Racial Violence in Manchester Schools*, Manchester: Manchester City Council. Also known as the 'Burnage High School Inquiry' or the 'Macdonald Report'. Summarized with extracts in an 8-page special report in the *Manchester Evening News*, 25 April 1988.

Marks, J. (1986) 'Education Policies on Race: A Case Study', in D. O'Keefe (ed.) *The Wayward Curriculum: A Cause for Parents' Concern*, London: Social Affairs Unit.

Mines, H. (1989) 'A review: English 5–11', *Issues in Race and Education*, Spring.

Minhas, R. (1989) 'Anti-racist Education: what future?' *Issues in Race and Education*, Spring.

Modgil, S. Verma, G., Mallick, D., and Modgil, C. (eds) (1986) *Multicultural Education: The Interminable Debate*, London: Falmer Press.

Multicultural Education Review, Birmingham: City of Birmingham Education Department, Multicultural Education Review, The Bordesley Centre, Stratford Road, Birmingham B11 1AR.

Multicultural Teaching, Stoke-on-Trent: Trentham Books Ltd, 30 Wenger Crescent, Trentham, Stoke-on-Trent ST4 8LE.

Multi-Ethnic Education Review, London: ILEA Multi-Ethnic Inspectorate, Room 468, County Hall, London SE1 7AB.

Multiracial Education, Walsall: National Anti-Racist Movement in Education, (NAME) P.O. Box 9, Walsall, West Midlands WS1 3SF.

National Anti-Racist Movement in Education (1985) *NAME on Swann*, Walsall: National Anti-Racist Movement in Education, P.O. Box 9, Walsall, West Midlands WS1 3SF.

National Curriculum Council (1988) *English for Ages 5–11*, York: National Curriculum Council, 15–17 New Street, York YO1 2RA.

National Curriculum Council (1989) *English 5–11 in the National Curriculum*, York: National Curriculum Council, 15–17 New Street, York YO1 2RA.

National Union of Teachers (1978) *Race, Education and Intelligence: A teacher's guide to the facts and issues*, London: National Union of Teachers.

National Union of Teachers (1982) *Education for a Multi-cultural Society: Evidence to the Swann Committee of Inquiry submitted by the National Union of Teachers*, London: National Union of Teachers.

National Union of Teachers (1982) *In Black and White: Guidelines for Teachers on Racial Stereotyping in Textbooks and Learning Materials*, London: National Union of Teachers.

National Union of Teachers (1984) *Combating Racism in Schools, A Union Policy Statement: guidance for members*, London: National Union of Teachers.

National Union of Teachers (1985) *Prejudice Plus Power: Challenging Racist Assumptions*, London:National Union of Teachers.

National Union of Teachers (1986) *Education for Equality: the National Union of Teachers' response to the Swann Report*, London: National Union of Teachers.

Neuberger, J. (1986) 'Hatred as a Moral Virtue: on the latest group diatribe from the anti-anti-racists', *Times Educational Supplement*, 5 Dec.

Nixon, J. (1985) *A Teacher's Guide to Multicultural Education*, Oxford: Blackwell.

O'Hear, A. (1989) *Who Teaches the Teachers? A contribution to public debate*, London: Social Affairs Unit.

O'Keefe, B. (1986) *Faith, Culture and the Dual System*, London: Falmer Press.

O'Keefe, D. (ed.) (1986) *The Wayward Curriculum: A Cause for Parents' Concern*, London: Social Affairs Unit.

Palmer, F. (1986) *Anti-Racism: An Assault on Education and Value*, Nottingham, Sherwood Press.

Race and Immigration, Runnymede Trust, 11 Princelet Street, London E1 6ZH.

Race Today, Race Today Collective, 165 Railton Road, London, SE24 0LY.

Richardson, R. (1985) 'Each and Every School: responding, reviewing, planning and doing'. *Multicultural Teaching* III (2), spring.

Richardson, R. (1988) 'Farewell to Racial Equality', *Times Educational Supplement*, 26 Feb.

Runnymede Trust (1985) *'Education For All': A summary of the Swann report on the education of ethnic minority children*, London: Runnymede Trust, 178 North Gower Street, London NW1 2NB.

Sarup, M. (1982) *Education, State and Crisis: A Marxist Perspective*, London: Routledge and Kegan Paul.

Sarup, M. (1986) *The Politics of Multiracial · Education*, London: Routledge and Kegan Paul.

Scarman, Lord (1981) *The Scarman Report: The Brixton Disorders, 10–12*

April 1981, London: Her Majesty's Stationery Office. Reprinted with Preface by Lord Scarman, 1986, London: Pelican.

Searchlight, Searchlight Publishing Limited, 37B New Cavendish Street, London W1M 8JR.

Sexton, S. (1987) *Our Schools – A Radical Policy*, London: Institute for Economic Affairs.

Sexton, S. (ed.) (1988) *GCSE: A Critical Analysis*, London: Institute for Economic Affairs.

Shaw, B. (1986) 'Teacher Training: The Misdirection of British Teaching', in D. O'Keefe (ed.) *The Wayward Curriculum: A Cause for Parents' Concern*, London: Social Affairs Unit.

Sherman, A. (1988) Chapter in S. Sexton (ed.) *GCSE: A Critical Analysis*, London: Institute for Economic Affairs.

Simon, R. (1982) *Gramsci's Political Thought: An Introduction*, London: Lawrence and Wishart.

Straker-Welds, M. (ed.) (1984) *Education for a Multicultural Society: Case Studies in ILEA Schools*, London: Bell and Hyman.

Swann, M. (1985) *Education for All: The Report of the Committee of Inquiry into the Education of Children from Ethnic Minority Groups*, London: Her Majesty's Stationery Office. Also known as the 'Swann Report'.

Trend, M. (1988) 'How Teachers Learn', *Spectator*, 15 Oct.

Troyna, B. (ed.) (1987) *Racial Inequality in Education*, London: Tavistock.

Troyna, B. and Ball, W. (1983) 'Multicultural education policies: are they worth the paper they're written on?, *Times Educational Supplement*, 9 Dec.

Twitchin, J. and Demuth, C. (1985) *Multi-Cultural Education: Views from the Classroom*, revised edn, London: BBC.

Verma, G. (1989) *Education for all: a landmark in pluralism*, London, Falmer Press.

Welsh Office (1984) *Initial Teacher Training: Approval of Courses*, Circular 21/84, Cardiff: Her Majesty's Stationery Office.

Wilby, P. (1988) 'Rag-Bags against Racism', *Independent*, 19 May.

Willis, P. (1978) *Learning to Labour: How Working Class Kids get Working Class Jobs*, London: Saxon House.

Wright, C. (1985) 'The Influence of School Processes on the Educational Opportunities of Children of West Indian Origin', *Multicultural Teaching* IV (1), Autumn.